Oh Promise Me

But Put It in Writing

OTHER BOOKS BY PAUL P. ASHLEY

Cases on Business Law • CO-AUTHOR (1929–1935)

Essentials of Libel (1948–1956)

Say It Safely: Legal Limits in Publishing, Radio, and Television, 4th rev. ed. (1969; *1st ed.,* 1956)

You and Your Will, 2nd ed. (1978; *1st ed.,* 1975)

Oh Promise Me

But Put It in Writing

Living-together agreements without,
before, during, and after marriage

Paul P. Ashley

McGRAW-HILL BOOK COMPANY

New York   St. Louis   San Francisco   Auckland   Bogotá
Düsseldorf   Johannesburg   London   Madrid
Mexico   Montreal   New Delhi   Panama
Paris   São Paulo   Singapore
Sydney   Tokyo   Toronto

Library of Congress Cataloging in Publication Data

Ashley, Paul Pritchard, 1896–
  Oh promise me . . . but put it in writing.

  1. Antenuptial contracts—United States.
2. Unmarried couples—Legal status, laws, etc.—United
States. 3. Husband and wife—United States. I. Title.
KF529.A83   346'.73'016   77-24904
ISBN 0-07-002409-X

1234567890   MUBP   7654321098

*The editors for this book were W. Hodson Mogan and Joan Zseleczky,
the designer was Naomi Auerbach, and the production supervisor
was Teresa F. Leaden. It was set in Electra
by The Fuller Organization, Inc.*

Printed by The Murray Printing Company and bound by The Book Press.

To Mary and Kay

Contents

Preface   ix

1. The Betrothal 1

Formalities, Past and Present   2
Good Faith   6
"Heart Balm" Suits   9
Return of Presents   14
Filiation Suits   18

2. Prenuptial Agreements 21

First Marriages   22
Subsequent Marriages   26
A Checklist for Prenuptial Agreements   29
Day-to-Day Details   36
Religious Predilections; Personal Conduct   38

3. The Marriage Contract 45

Nature of the Contract   47
Inherent Rights and Duties   48
Termination of Contract   51

4. Quasi and Same-Sex Marriages 61

Caveat—Warning   63
Heterosexual Arrangements   67
  A trust relationship   69
  A partnership relationship   70
  A cooperative enterprise   70
  Joint-ownership agreements   70
  Support of children   71
  Contracts regarding wills   71
Homosexual Marriages   72
  Legality of homosexual marriage contracts   72
  Other contracts between homosexuals   76

5. Agreements during Marriage 79

Ownerships   80
Loans   85
Partnerships and Joint Ventures   86
Employment   89
Recordkeeping; Taxes   90

6. Estate Planning; Trusts 93

Wills   94
Merged Families   96
Transfers of Property; Taxes; Insurance   98
Trusts   98
Power of Attorney   100

7. Property Settlement and Separation Agreements 107

Validity   108
Agreements Designed to be Permanent   110
Separation with Hope of Reunion   124
Alimony   126

8. Postdissolution Contracts 129

Custody and Support of Children   130
Agreements to Modify Alimony   133
Property Rights and Obligations   134

Index   137

Preface

This is a fireside chat, not a legal discussion. The objectives are easily stated: (1) to describe the nature of marriage promises, before, during, and after, (2) to review living-together arrangements whether heterosexual or homosexual, and (3) to do so briefly but in sufficient detail to enable the reader intelligently to ask: "Is it possible that *before* we are married or begin living together there should be a written treaty regarding property rights and obligations?" Or to ask the equivalent question later, whether the sailing be calm or tempestuous.

I believe that frequently prenuptial contracts are not considered because of an emotional feeling—"They are too businesslike. Crass commercial conversations should not occur between lovers. We will be able to discuss and agree on financial affairs."

But this is not always true. Spouses frequently find it extremely difficult, even impossible, to plan together and concur in regard to money matters.

A marriage contract is not magic. It cannot automatically solve all problems, particularly monthly budgets where income is not plentiful. As I have watched marriages come and go over many years—between clients, where I am supposed to know the ultimate facts which led to discord, and between friends and neighbors, where there is a general knowledge of the debacle—I am convinced that in many instances a proper agreement might have prevented fatal dissension or at least made the separation much smoother for all concerned.

You may wonder why a lawyer who enjoys writing should produce a book like this, instead of a tome intended for the profession—complete with quotations from and citations to leading decisions of appellate courts, texts, encyclopedias, law reviews, and other material pertaining to legal questions. The answer is that these books are not readily available and are not easily understood by the very people who may be most affected. Lawyers have plenty of books. I think the greater service is conveying legal possibilities to the people on the firing line.

A thank-you is due to the Bancroft-Whitney Company of San Francisco, California, and to the Lawyers Co-operative Publishing Company of Rochester, New York, for their gracious permission to follow the language of their excellent publications—*American Jurisprudence* and *American Law Reports Annotated*—without making special mention of it in each of the score or so of instances where I have used their material.

Paul P. Ashley

Oh Promise Me
But Put It in Writing

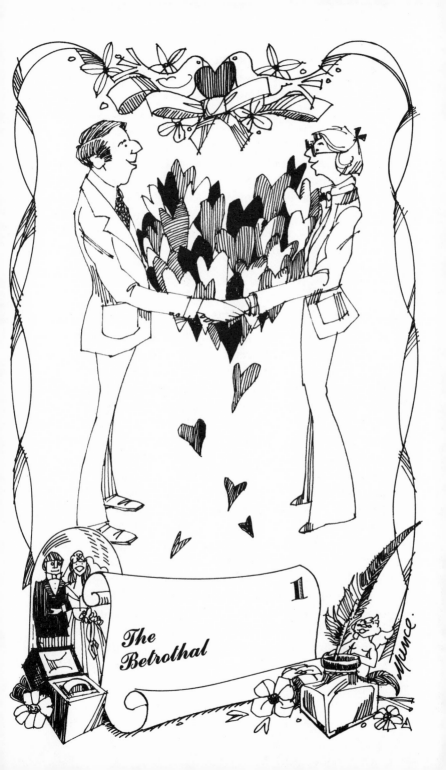

1

The
Betrothal

The betrothal—the pledge between the prospective bride and bridegroom to marry or, in parts of the world, the agreement between families that a son and daughter shall marry—is the first in the hierarchy of marriage contracts. In importance, it ranks close to the celebration of the marriage or the gloom of a separation agreement. Yet, especially in America, it is often (if not usually) entered into secretly, in an environment and under emotional conditions not conducive to the sound judgment customarily deemed essential to the making of vital contracts. What astute person, for example, would consider it sensible to decide on an important business transaction while parked romantically beside a moonlit lake?

Formalities, past and present

There have been and are many betrothal practices. At one time, Rome had a lottery for lovers. Young women wrote their names on slips of paper which were deposited in an open drum. Interested swains reached in and took one. Today's advertisements tell of matching by data processing machines. There are no studies demonstrating that one system brings greater long-span happiness than the other.

At the most exalted levels, ministers of state may be intermediaries. The infant Mary, Queen of Scots, is a celebrated example of arranged betrothals. The marriage treaty between Mary and Edward, then Prince of Wales and later Edward VI, was signed at Greenwich in July 1543. Mary was about seven months old. The covenant guaranteed that when she became ten years of age she would be placed in the keeping of Henry VIII, father of the presumptive groom.

This unromantic betrothal was abrogated because of the obvious aim of Henry VIII, the potential father-in-law, to annex the Crown of Scotland forthwith (not waiting for a baby to grow to marriageable age) supplemented by pressure from Mary's mother, a member of the powerful Guise family of France. Not unnaturally, the mother consistently favored and worked for a French marriage.

When almost six, the young Queen was again betrothed, this time to the Dauphin Francis. She was taken to Paris to begin ten years' training under the tutelage of Catherine de Medicis, Queen of France. The juggling of Mary's betrothal was not untypical. At birth, highly placed infants became pawns of state, and often their arranged marriages furthered international stability.

Between peasants and royalty, family considerations frequently play a part; the advantage of merging adjoining farms is a classic example. As put by Will and Ariel Durant in their volume *The Age of Reason Begins*, in the era of Elizabeth I, "most marriages were arranged after a mutual courtship of properties." But in this last half of the twentieth century, in the United States, personal "negotiations" between sweethearts are usual and take precedence over family considerations. In our country, courtship almost always must be person to person: the general rule is that a contract to pay a third person for arranging a marriage is illegal.

Traditionally, the betrothal agreement involved protocol, ceremony, and with lofty families, pomp and circumstance. Even today in some cultures, betrothal agreements are customarily made without participation by the principals—the prospective bride and groom. As to humble families, the arrangements may be agreed upon between the parents (perhaps using a marriage broker), the bride and groom first meeting at the wedding. And, of course, the pact may be made between the man and the maiden's parents. Jacob dealt directly with Laban, the crafty father of Rachel, and worked a total of fourteen years for her hand.

American law requires no formalities in respect to the betrothal—the basic pledge to marry—but any agreement predicated upon the lovers' promise must meet the legal requirements of the jurisdiction (the state) where made.

Three hundred years ago (1677), in England, there was

enacted the "Statute in Prevention of Frauds and Perjuries," now commonly called the statute of frauds. With variations, it is found in the laws of every state. It requires that certain contracts be in writing—for instance, any contract for the sale and purchase of real estate. Any oral agreement, promise, or undertaking made upon consideration of marriage is invalid, that is, if you will marry me, I will do so and so—usually involving property and finance. The actual *mutual promise to marry* is expressly excepted. It may be made orally, in the rose garden or during a Strauss waltz.

Logically, there must be a betrothal contract preceding the marriage ceremony. Currently, in almost all states, the optimistic couple must or is supposed to secure a license from a public official and (in most) wait a designated number of days before entering into the contract of marriage. Some states require medical certifications. Even when a compliant judge waives the statutory standby period and permits or even performs an immediate ceremony, there must have been at least a short betrothal agreement prior to applying to the functionaries at the courthouse.

Over the centuries and in different parts of the world, there have been many betrothal customs—some of them merging into the myths reaching back to the days when the gods metamorphosed into human beings and mated with earthlings. Competitive racing for the bride had delightful variations. In one, it is said the prospective bride was handed a heavy whip. Then she fled, her lovers chasing after her. Whether on horseback or on foot she could use the lash to fend off those who followed. Expectedly, the one not whipped away won the race, demonstrating an early assertion of equal rights for women.

This custom brings to mind the familiar German folktale. The prosperous village tailor thought Fritz to be the best tailor in the area, therefore destined to marry his daughter, Gretel, and carry on the business. But the beautiful Gretel loved a young tailor named Hans, whose skills, the father believed, were inferior to those of Fritz. Gretel proposed a race to decide the quandary. Papa would design a cloak and furnish the suitors with cloth and identical patterns. Gretel would sit between the contestants, threading the needles of each. The threads she put into the needle of Fritz were longer than those given Hans. So to the surprise of all but Gretel, Hans won. Each stitch required less movement of his arm; hence he was faster. A betrothal agreement had been reached with parental acquiescence.

At one stage the Catholic Church declared that females between the ages of seven and twelve and males between the ages of seven and fourteen could be betrothed, but not married, and that betrothals were to be published. The Church became distressed because impetuous young people considered a betrothal as justifying cohabitation in advance of marriage which might be years away. To this very day, one or both of the contracting parties may prefer to have the sanction of the church of their choice and the publishing of banns in advance of marriage, sometimes with notable formality.

There is an exception to the logical need of a betrothal agreement, whether made by the heads of the contracting families, or through go-betweens, or by the prospective bride and groom. It is the traditional "common-law" marriage. The parties may simply drift into living together, or between themselves make sacred vows to do so permanently, and then continue their relationship for a long time. *They hold themselves out as husband and wife.* In the states where common-law marriages are recognized, these are real marriages. If children are born, they are legitimate. The parties may accumulate property. The children may inherit.

In frontier days distances were great, transportation was slow, and it might be very difficult for the betrothed to journey to a place where licenses were issued. During this period, our states were more prone to recognize common-law marriages as legal than was the common law of England.

Fewer than a third of the states still permit common-law marriages. I do not list those jurisdictions where today it would be predictable that the court would rule a common-law marriage valid, because (1) tomorrow, by legislation or court decision, the rule may change and (2) in every state it is better for those who wish to be lawfully married to be married in the fashion which is there orthodox.

So instead of giving a list which may be outmoded by the time this is in print, my advice to couples who believe they are, or wish to be, bound by a *legally valid* common-law marriage is to secure a written opinion from a solid lawyer. The lawyer's advice may be: "All is serene as long as you live in this state." Or it may be: "Immediately formalize your relationship with a legally recognized ceremony." The latter may be performed in a distant county seat, before a judge or justice of the peace, with the clerk and bailiff as witnesses, with minimal chance of any home town publicity or even knowledge of the reason for the trip if the couple wishes to maintain secrecy.

Good faith

When entering into a betrothal agreement—the glamour of romance notwithstanding—the affianced man and woman owe each other an obligation of good faith in respect to mundane property matters and other important facts of life. It is quite possible that Mary would not have agreed to marry Jonathan *if* he had frankly told her how much he owes on the Coupe de Ville and the tenuous nature of his job. Indeed, the root "troth" means fidelity, truth, verity, as in "by my troth."

The law has a broad term which comprehends these strict obligations of honesty and good faith. It is called a "fiduciary relationship." From the moment flirtation and courting develop into serious negotiations—the possible desirability of marriage in the minds of both—there comes into being a fiduciary relationship. This means mutual confidence and trust which call for the exercise of candor and sincerity in all significant matters. Assets owned and fiscal obligations should be revealed with a basic accuracy which would do credit to an accountant, though not necessarily duplicating his detail.

As is almost always so when broad legal rules are concerned, there are exceptions. Some courts draw a distinction between the duty of full disclosures before and after the betrothal. Other courts consider such a distinction unrealistic. The Supreme Court of Maryland remarked:

> It would seem to be anomalous to say that the instant before a woman signs an ante-nuptial agreement she deals with her prospective husband as a stranger, and he with her, but that in the twinkling of an eye, after they append their signatures to the instrument, a confidential relation exists between them. In most instances such a conclusion is not based on the realities of life, but is more the product of fantasy.
>
> We cannot subscribe to the doctrine that a man and woman, under such circumstances, are to be treated like merchant princes dealing with each other, each implemented with the exacting and hard instruments of commercialism.

A marriage of convenience may call for a modification of the rule demanding disclosure. There, as one court elegantly said, the business judgment of the parties is "unlikely to be clouded with the prehymeneal ardor and tenderness" ordinarily associated with betrothals.

Contrary, it seems to me, to the good-faith doctrine, there is a general rule to the effect that concealment of a previous marriage which was terminated by divorce is an insufficient reason for annulment. The Supreme Court of New Hampshire recently faced that problem. The wife's second husband brought suit for an annulment, alleging that she had represented herself as a widow when actually she was a divorcée and her first husband was still living at the time of the remarriage. The plaintiff husband was a faithful member of the Roman Catholic Church; it was against his religious convictions to marry a divorcée whose prior husband was still living.

The New Hampshire court quoted and recognized the general rule, even though the first husband had obligingly died before trial, thus making the controversy moot.

I do not venture advice as to when previous indiscretions should be revealed—unless somewhere there is a child to support. But certainly, despite cases like that from New Hampshire, previous marriages should not be kept a secret. This is definitely so when there is a former spouse claiming, or who might belatedly claim, alimony or an interest in property. An embarrassing family situation should not be hidden—perhaps a relative in jail or extremely difficult parents or siblings. Personal physical infirmities should not be camouflaged too much. Any such cover-up would be a breach of the fiduciary relationship.

Because utmost good faith is required, there is a presumption that the intended wife was not fully informed by her wealthy fiancé if the prenuptial agreement fails to make adequate provision for her in relation to the circumstances of the prospective husband. The same holds true for a man with a wealthy fiancée.

Not everyone is eligible for betrothal. The law must say that a promise by one already married to marry someone else is void. Nor is the betrothal good when between persons forbidden to marry because of consanguinity—meaning kinship, blood relationship, descent from a common ancestor not sufficiently remote. Prohibitions based on relationship vary greatly among states. Then there are questions of age and of physical or mental competence, again to be decided under the law of the state which has jurisdiction of the parties. One lives in Minnesota; the other in Michigan; the betrothal promises were made on a palm-studded beach in Florida. If there is any question as to competency, it is an "ask your lawyer" dilemma.

This discussion of financial frankness and open honesty in respect to the betrothal applies with equal force to prenuptial agreements and to marriage contracts, as well as to postnuptial property agreements and separation and dissolution agreements. In short, whenever a prospective bride and groom or husband and wife are making a covenant, principles of good faith should be present in all their dealings. There will be no need to repeat this basic rule as we move from one type of contract to another.

Heart-balm suits

Lawsuits, often called "heart-balm" suits, based on breach of contract to marry are infrequent. Indeed in some states* legal redress is not available, though wars have been fought and revolutions have blazed because a duke repudiated his promised princess or vice versa.

Even in the relatively few states which bar heart-balm suits, judges are not reluctant to bypass the inhibitory statute when there has been a gross unfairness and the attorney for the injured party can concoct a theory which ties into an authoritative decision upholding the client's position. Take, for example, the following case, which was tried in New Jersey, where there is a law abolishing actions to recover damages for breach of contract to marry. An overly canny lawyer employed an overly trusting secretary. They made a novel contract to marry, he meanwhile withholding part of her weekly stipend. In due course she quit her job. He refused to marry her or to pay her the portion of the salary which he had retained. He felt secure because of the statute forbidding suits based on breach of a betrothal contract. Her attorney urged that the fundamental contract was one of employment, not mutual promises to marry. The court agreed; the secretary recovered the money which had been withheld.

* Presently: Alabama, California, Florida, Indiana, Massachusetts, Michigan, New Hampshire, New Jersey, New York, and Pennsylvania.

Usually, in the United States, the end of an engagement results in no more than a ring returned and a torrent of gossip. When it is said that Judson and Henrietta have "broken their engagement," it commonly refers to a situation where the *two* parties have abandoned their contract. One may have been the aggressor (she returned his ring) and the other brokenhearted because of the change in status. But, probably after tears and attempts to reconcile, they both finally acquiesce in the proposition that their agreement to marry each other should terminate. This sort of conclusion of the once happy relationship does not lead to litigation.

But if, as has been said, the betrothal contract is a lawful, legal contract, damages may flow from a unilateral repudiation. "Unilateral" means by one of them over the objection of the other.

Let us suppose that Lucille, a young widow with two children, lives in Cleveland. She owns a modest home and has a responsible job with Cleveland Electric Illuminating Company. She falls in love with and becomes engaged to a man from Dallas, age about forty, wealthy. He gives her a diamond, carats sufficient to do credit to a Texan.

They plan a summer wedding so the children's schooling will not be interrupted midterm. She sells her house and disposes of most of her furniture. At the office they give her a going away party and presents.

Then comes the bomb. The Texan writes that he met a woman from Hollywood, fell head-over heels in love with her, and that they were married the day before yesterday.

Is not the Texan guilty of a breach of contract legally entitling Lucille to recover substantial damages? Note that, in contrast to many forsaken women, she suffered special, provable monetary loss in addition to humiliation and emotional distress. What would you award if you were on the jury?

Lucille's is not a lawsuit against a third party (the other woman) for alienation of affections. Though long recognized, actions of that sort are not now favored, and in some jurisdictions they are forbidden or dramatically limited.* Lucille's suit is for breach of a lawful agreement. Relying on the Texan's promises, she radically changed her position, parted with her house, gave up a permanent job with seniority, and a good, though possibly lonely, way of life. Perhaps the jury should be generous.

In the three dozen states where heart-balm suits are permitted, they are not to be viewed lightly. By way of damages, the plaintiff may allege and, subject to the usual rules of evidence, will be given an opportunity to prove mental anguish and humiliation; damages to health and reputation; loss of another opportunity to marry; loss of pecuniary advantages, including potential participation in an estate which defendant is destined to inherit; loss from giving up a job (as did Lucille) and expenditures in anticipation of the coming marriage; investment losses (Lucille sold her house); and damages due to unmarried pregnancy and abortion. Obviously the last is unavailable when the woman walks out on the man and he is the plaintiff.

There can be no precise rule. The courts, however, generally hold that the plaintiff shall have an opportunity to prove damages of the sort just enumerated. Illustrations abound. A Kansas court emphasized the "sense of disgrace" and "loss of reputation" suffered by an abandoned woman. A Delaware court was compassionate when viewing the plight of a music teacher who dismissed her pupils and expectantly invested her savings in a trousseau: the deserter was ordered to pay, plenty. An eminent judge stressed the value of the "social advantages which would have accrued to her as his wife." The worth of services rendered the defendant promissor in reliance on the promise of marriage is usually recoverable as are damages for premarital sexual relations induced by the broken promise, even though monetary reimburse-

* Including Alabama, California, Colorado, Connecticut, Florida, Indiana, Louisiana, Maryland, Michigan, Nevada, New Jersey, New York, Pennsylvania, Wyoming, and Washington.

ment would not be allowed based on seduction of an adult *not* tied to a betrothal contract. After all, the person acquiesced, perhaps enthusiastically.

So there may be a serious suit ending in a jury award against the guilty party unless there are ameliorating circumstances. In some states, punitive damages (damages to punish, not merely to recompense) are allowed. They would be based on proof of fraud or malice on the part of the defendant; wanton or ruthless conduct, thus unnecessarily wounding the plaintiff's feelings; or other activities repugnant to the mores of the county where the suit is tried.

Granted that heart-balm suits are rare, people of means should not assume that breach of a betrothal agreement is no more than an emotional upset. However, there are occasional rulings by trial judges who consider themselves "advanced thinkers" which give support to a trivial-trauma theory. Recently, in a state which has *not* banned suits for breach of promise to marry, a judge faced these facts: The engaged couple had purchased a house and wedding rings. The woman had listed her home for sale and had sold her furniture at auction. They had arranged for a church and minister. Then, without cause, he abandoned her. The modern-minded judge stated that: (1) marriage engagements are not what they used to be, (2) the defendant had broken no laws by refusing to marry the plaintiff, (3) "in this modern age" it is not likely that a couple will view an engagement as a legally binding contract.

Of course the defendant broke no law in a criminal sense. But could a judge be more ridiculous than when he rules that a widow with two children who sells her furniture at auction, lists her house for sale, helps buy rings and arrange for church and clergyman, was not relying on the promises of her Romeo? Perhaps she has appealed, and the supreme court of the state will reverse this inequitable judgment.

In heart-balm suits, it is usually the men who are the defendants. The great preponderance of reported cases are brought by women. As women become more active and successful in economic affairs, it is likely that some current may flow in the opposite direction.

Of course there are defenses which may shield the accused, in whole or in part. "In mitigation" is a common term when referring to a partial defense. Defenses, if provable, include: a fundamental lack of affection, one for the other; ill health, particularly impotency; a history of insanity in plaintiff's family discovered by defendant after the engagement; plaintiff's bad character, or unchaste and indecent conduct, also tardily discovered; and plaintiff's marriage or engagement to another person before the day of trial (though it is rather insulting to the new spouse for his or her partner to persist in a heart-balm suit against a former fiancé!). Pressing a heart-balm suit *after* marriage to a third party sounds ridiculous, but there are such controversies in the law reports.

In an action based on breach of contract to marry, there are three basic questions:

Item 1. Was there a promise to marry on which plaintiff was entitled to rely?

Item 2. Has defendant repudiated it without justification?

Item 3. What price in dollars should be put upon each allowable element of damage suffered by the injured party?

All of them may be very difficult to answer.

Item 1: Was there a promise to marry upon which the plaintiff was entitled to rely? It may be difficult to prove according to legal standards unless there was correspondence. As everyone knows, most promises to marry are made when the lovers are alone. If the defendant has told others of the promise, the statements are admissible as evidence. But the defendant is not bound by what the plaintiff has said to third parties when the defendant was not present to hear it and be able to contradict it, if false. Asserting that an overeager plaintiff had acted prematurely, a defendant might truthfully deny any knowledge of the preparation and mailing of the wedding invitations.

Proof of repudiation, the first phase of item 2, should not be a serious problem. The defendant would not be in court if willing to go through with the marriage. However, even this is subject to a qualification: What if, for example, after the wedding invitations have been mailed with his knowledge and cooperation and the bride's plans completed, the faithless groom told her he had changed his mind? Then later, he changes it again and says he would like to marry her, or at least is willing to do so.

The second phase of item 2, "without justification," must face the hurdles which the defendant may raise in mitigation or as a complete defense. Should the plaintiff be awarded damages if, after making the contract to marry, the defendant learns that there is an unfortunate record of insanity in plaintiff's family?

Item 3: The value of the broken contract in terms of dollars is related to defendant's financial status. That is contrary to the usual rule in fixing damages, whether based on breach of contract or negligent injury to the plaintiff. If the defendant negligently smashed your fender, the law says he or she must pay the cost of repairs plus, perhaps, a realistic sum to compensate you for loss of necessary use of your car. Not more because the defendant is rich or less because the defendant is poor.

But, in a breach of promise suit, the financial situation of the defendant enters directly as an element of damage. Sometimes, the financial situation of the defendant's family may have a bearing. A young defaulting groom without, as yet, a sou in his own name recently lost his father through death, and the estate is in probate. The will may show funds which will flow to him. The elements of damage may be hard to appraise.

Return of presents

There is another type of legal proceeding which may stem from the breach of a betrothal contract. It is a claim for the return of valuable presents. Such cases are difficult for a judge or a jury to decide. For the sake of simplicity, let us pretend that all important gifts come from the prospective groom, although that is not necessarily so. The judicial process must decide: Were the presents given as an inducement to the woman to marry him? Or were they no more than generous gestures from a friend or suitor, not conditioned on marriage? Or were they in appreciation of sexual favors by the woman, the then wary man prudently or unscrupulously—as one views his conduct—refraining from any suggestion of marriage? The members of the jury might differ.

At long last, the man softened and proposed marriage. The woman accepted. He gave her a magnificent engagement ring, a fitting apex to the valuable jewelry and furs he had lavished upon her. Soon *she* changed her mind, but refused to return any of his gifts. A ladylike good taste cannot be the test; manners differ with social strata. The law must apply to all, regardless of breeding.

In a case hinging on the distinction between an engagement ring and a dinner ring, a New York court made a decision worthy of Solomon. The engagement ring, it was decided, must be returned to the jilted fiancé. The woman may keep the dinner ring. The rationale was this: The engagement ring was clearly tied to marriage; it was a notice to the world that she would be married to the donor. In contrast, the dinner ring was not clearly predicated on marriage. It may have no greater legal significance than a generous birthday present.

A number of decisions from various states make this distinction. An engagement ring is unique; it must be returned. As to other gifts, the answer may be yes or it may be no, depending on the proved circumstances and the philosophy of the law of the jurisdiction in respect to heart-balm suits generally. Some courts, which by statute are compelled to refuse to entertain a suit brought for recompense for a broken heart, will nevertheless direct that presents, particularly an engagement ring, be returned.

The usual rule is different in respect to clearly courtship gifts—those given *prior* to a betrothal. The decisions usually say that unless there has been deceit or undue influence on the part of the donee (the person to whom the gift is given), anyone who makes a gift during the courtship period irrevocably parts with the property. This rule has been applied strictly, if not harshly, and should not be forgotten by those inclined to gild their courtship with gold.

In Kansas, a man seventy-eight years of age deeded land to a woman in her forties in a futile attempt to persuade her to marry him. After he abandoned his courtship as a lost cause, he brought suit to secure the return of his property. There was no proof that the venerable Lochinvar was mentally incapacitated or that the lady had exerted undue influence upon him. The Kansas court reasoned that "undue influence" in a legal sense is more than being so fascinating to a man thirty years older that he deeds you valuable lands. At that stage in their relationship, she did not have a fiduciary duty to protect him against himself.

A Quaker State court held that an equitable proceeding to force a reconveyance of real property was not barred by the heart-balm statute of that commonwealth, nor by a kindred law barring actions to recover gifts given in contemplation of marriage. Unmarried, the parties lived together as husband and wife. She had promised to marry him as soon as he was divorced from his present wife. When the divorce was completed, the paramour repudiated her promise but insisted on keeping the land he had deeded to her. The Pennsylvania judge ordered her to deed it back to him.

The language of another Pennsylvania court is so delightful that I must follow it. The name of the case is *Pavlicic* v. *Vogtsberger*. The learned judge reasoned that a gift given by a man to a woman on condition that she embark with him on the sea of matrimony is no different from a gift based on the condition that she sail with him on any other sea. If, after accepting the provisional gratuity, she refused to leave the harbor—if the anchor of contractual performance sticks in the sands of irresolution and procrastination—the gift must be restored to the donor. This would be especially true when the lady not only refuses to sail with him but, flauntingly, walks up the gangplank of another ship, arm in arm with the donor's rival.

Going back a century, the learned Joseph Strutt (1749–1802) states that by civil law gifts given at betrothal could be recovered by the parties, if the marriage did not take place. But only conditionally. For if the man "had had a kiss for his money, he should lose one-half of that which he gave." Yet with the woman it is otherwise, for, "kissing or not kissing, whatever she gave, she may ask and have it again." However, these rules extended "only to gloves, rings, bracelets and such-like small wares."

Looking beyond emotional trauma and fringe issues, two essentials to the recovery of a gift are: (1) proof that the present was made conditionally, in contemplation of marriage and (2) proof that the termination of the engagement was not the fault of the one who seeks to retrieve the gift.

What if the performance of the contract is thwarted by the death of the prospective bride with a costly engagement ring on her finger? Does the ring become an asset of her estate, or should it be returned to the formerly prospective groom? Court decisions sustain an argument either way. I believe it should be returned.

Third-party donors of gifts, to one or both members of an engaged couple, occasionally bring suit to recoup the gift, if there is no marriage. For example: In Maryland, Sara's father deposited substantial sums to the joint credit of Sara and Harry, who were engaged. Shortly Harry's attachment to Sara waned, but his love for the money continued. He refused to repay father, who brought suit against Harry and won.

A Georgia mother loaned a diamond ring to her son, who gave it to his beloved when they became engaged. The girl broke the engagement but held fast to the ring. Mother brought suit, demanding its return. She prevailed.

Bankruptcy proceedings may interfere. Acting in good

faith, but shortly before becoming bankrupt, a gallant gave his betrothed a valuable diamond ring. The trustee in bankruptcy demanded the ring of the woman, who refused to give it up. The court held that she must either surrender the ring or pay its value.

Filiation suits

Beyond litigation concerning things material hovers the possibility of a filiation suit. In legal parlance, it is a proceeding asking for a judicial assignment of an illegitimate child to a designated man as his or her father. The woman hails her former betrothed into court and says: "He is the father of my child born seven months after our engagement was terminated. He denies paternity." These are unpleasant proceedings. If he had admitted fatherhood, there would be no need of such a suit. So it may be presumed that he will persist in his denial.

There lies the child in a crib in view of judge and jury. Defendant admits intercourse during the period of the engagement. His only biological defense is that his fiancée was sleeping with at least one other man. Blood tests are inconclusive. She indignantly denies the charge, asserting that she bedded with the defendant only because they were engaged and she was confident that they would be married.

It is impossible to know in advance how a judge or jury will analyze the evidence. A different result may be forthcoming in a conservative, churchgoing county than might have been obtained in a more ambivalent metropolitan area. As is expectable, a promise by a married person to marry after the death or divorce of a present spouse is illegal.

It is arguable, if not demonstrable, that our present laissez-faire policy in respect to entering into betrothal agreements is in part responsible for the accelerating divorce rate. Years ago, when the betrothal was a family and perhaps a church affair, with multiple threads to hold the couple together after marriage, the formal prenuptial agreement, described in the next chapter, was not as necessary as it has become today.

The boy and girl had known each other for a long time. So had their families. The roots of the new ménage dug deep in their community; lifelong friends attended the wedding and expected the bride and groom to succeed as husband and wife. It was correct, or at least possible, to write "a family wedding is a marriage of families." Now that would not often be true; for millions, that support no longer surrounds them.

During at least two generations, perhaps for the last three, people have been on the move. Corporations are perpetually shifting personnel from one city to another. Old ties are severed. For most young people, a constant, traditional neighborhood pressure upon the new family to make good has vanished.

This new era makes prenuptial contracts more important than they were in a more stable environment. They establish guidelines for the separation agreement (Chapter VII), if that tragedy comes.

HERS......
HIS......
HERS......

Hers
HIS

MINE
YOURS

OURS
MINE
YOURS

Mine
Thine

2

*Prenuptial
Agreements*

On the stern of a big tanker truck which blocks your passage on the highway appears the word "flammable." On the next truck in line is the word "inflammable." The meaning is the same.

When referring to contracts made in anticipation of marriage (property and other ancillary agreements; not the betrothal agreement, though predicated thereon), a familiar word is "antenuptial." Another is "prenuptial." Both "ante" and "pre" mean "before." With equal validity, they combine with literally hundreds of English words to show a time sequence; as "predawn" and "antebellum." But "ante" is more vulnerable to error. "Anti" sounds and looks almost the same; with one slip of a finger of the typist or typesetter we find "anti," meaning "against." A careful drafting of contracts should minimize opportunities for error. So here we will talk about "prenuptial" agreements, the reader realizing that elsewhere it may be written "antenuptial."

First marriages

Assuming candor and good faith, the courts generally uphold prenuptial property agreements freely and intelligently entered into between the prospective bride and groom. These agreements are regarded as conducive to marital tranquillity and to the avoidance of disputes about the ownership, use, and descent of property. And, of course, if property problems arise after marriage (see "Agreements during Marriage"), a friendly written treaty between husband and wife is far better than bickering and perhaps divorce—now often called dissolution.

When we observe first marriages of young people, few seem to require a prenuptial agreement. Usually neither has accumulated substantial investments. In the absence of inherited wealth or the probability of a large inheritance by one or both of them, there may seem no need of a prenuptial contract concerning property to supplement the nuptial vows.

However, the fact that relatively few first-timers do have a contract does not support an inference that there should not be more, many more. Let us imagine a pair recently graduated from college. To make the illustration stronger, add a graduate degree (a specialization) for one or both of them. The woman has a career very much in mind. A prenuptial agreement recognizing her ambition, and thereby implicitly her ability, might be in order. The expected vocation of one of them may be practicable in only a few cities, where facilities for proposed research are available. Suitable work for the other is feasible in many localities. Should their contract contain a provision to the effect that they will live in an area (perhaps name several possibilities) where opportunities to exploit the specialized training are open?

What, you ask, shall be put in the contract if the prospective bride and groom will both be limited geographically in respect to vocational advancement or even a first job? One must be near a great university with technical equipment; the other, where timber is farmed. Where will they live? If there is no answer, it may be better to know that harsh fact early and reexamine their suitability for each other.

Or assume a young couple, neither well educated. Both work. Both are determined that their family will be an example of the American Dream—a way of homelife for their children that is several levels above that of their immigrant grandparents. If inclined toward a written covenant, they should have one, based upon their hope for the future rather than on current assets.

Should not a woman in her twenties marrying a confirmed bachelor, age fifty, with considerable property and earning power, have a prenuptial formula to protect her if the mating of spring and fall should not meld? If a separation should come within a few years—when the wife is still young enough to secure a job easily—the judge might not give her a fair share of the fortune of her husband. So I suggest a prenuptial agreement might be prudent—to protect the rich husband from excessive demands and to enable the divorced wife (now age thirty) to continue to enjoy a way of life better than her earnings from an entry-level job would permit. But, as will be stressed shortly, their contract must not be so worded as to facilitate divorce.

Or suppose the ages of the young betrothed are comparable, but the financial state of their families is radically dissimilar. The man enjoys the backing of great wealth. His fiancée comes from a family close to the poverty level. If they marry, and particularly if they have children during their early twenties (or before), she may never learn skills which will bring a satisfactory financial return. He has a lucrative path ahead as a trainee for executive posts in a business owned by his family, plus the expectation of an inheritance. There will be an abundance for him and his brother and two sisters.

The divorce pattern in his social set, however, is at least as bad as the national average. Looking at the situation realistically and not romantically, should not the bride be protected if one day she should be ousted from or feel that she must escape from the jet-set way of life to which she has never become quite accustomed? And if the marriage should fail, should not the husband be protected against unreasonable claims far beyond ample provisions for the potential divorcée and the educational requirements of their children? Bluntly, should not he and his family have assurance that they will not be "bled," just as she should have assurance from them that generous provision will be made for her in the event of estrangement or the death of the husband? With a fairly worded contract as to the property and support in the event of disaster or death, there might be less financial tension between them, thus actually aiding in holding the marriage intact. And it should not be forgotten that, unless bound to her wealthy in-laws by mutual love for her children, upon the death of the scion she may be considered outside the elite and entitled to no more than a minimum financial settlement. Her statutory rights as a wife (often called "dower") may or may not protect her. Perhaps at the time of his death, only a trivial part of his family's fortune was actually vested in the young husband, that is, was really *owned* by him.

Reversing the illustration: A woman rich in her own right marries a delightful man whose vocational prognosis does not include high earnings. Might a premarital contract make easier a style of living above his income and give both peace of mind when discussing finances or planning trips?

It must be remembered that premarital contracts are not of public record like a deed or mortgage. They may be kept secret if those involved are discreet. If worse comes to worst, the public spectacle of a contested divorce may be avoided.

Premarital contracts need not be couched in stilted legalese—as though the contracting parties mistrusted each other. Shortly a contract will be quoted in full—in part to show provisions deemed suitable under the special circumstances (a second marriage), but also to exemplify the *tone* of any prenuptial agreement. Then will follow a comprehensive checklist against which to measure all prenuptial agreements. Proper covenants need not detract from the romance of the coming wedding.

Nevertheless, it must be remembered that traditionally a prenuptial agreement which facilitates a separation or divorce is contrary to public policy. Hence, if not carefully worded, an agreement may be unenforceable.

An application of this principle is found in the Ledoux case decided in Louisiana. By a marriage contract, husband Ledoux gave his wife some land and three slaves. His gift was subject to the condition that the property should be returned to him if she should predecease him "or in any manner or form be separated from him as her husband." The wife obtained a divorce on the grounds of adultery. The court said she could keep the land and slaves.

The most authoritative text statement is found in the *Restatement of the Law,* sponsored by the American Law Institute. It gives this illustration: John and Mary are about to marry and they enter into a prenuptial bargain providing that if they find it impossible to live together amicably and therefore separate, their respective property interests will be what they owned prior to their marriage. This bargain is illegal because it has a tendency to lead to separation. (It is also incomplete; what about property accumulated by their efforts after marriage?) This traditional concept of the "illegality" of such a contract seems to be fading.

Similarly, there have been contracts which provide that, in the event the parties separate for any cause, one spouse forfeits rights to certain property without regard to the issue of fault in causing the separation. Such a provision is promotive of separation and has been held contrary to public policy. Under the developing no-fault dissolution theories of terminating marriages (later discussed), the answer may be otherwise.

Subsequent marriages

When it is a subsequent, past-forty marriage, the probable desirability of a prenuptial agreement is even greater. The prospective bride and groom will have had more years within which to earn money and to inherit from deceased relatives. One or both may have received substantial sums from the estate of a spouse. The expectant second- or third-time prospective bride (or bridegroom) may have emerged exceedingly well from a divorce settlement.

So, not infrequently one or both have substantial properties. One or both may have children, and these children may be of greatly staggered ages. If there has been a divorce, there will be varying formulas as to support and visiting rights, seasoned by the financial stability and temperament of the divorced spouse.

A prenuptial property agreement, carefully and lovingly worked out between repeaters *before* the second or third marriage begins, may well prevent another wreck. It may properly include provisions for contributions to financial burdens outside the new family about to be formed, as well as covenants protecting each other.

Here follows (except that the names are fictitious) a complete contract included, as indicated, to illustrate language as well as substance.

PRENUPTIAL AGREEMENT

THIS AGREEMENT is entered into between ANN A. SMITH (Ann) presently of Evanston, Illinois, and JAMES B. HOWELL (James) of Portland, Maine. In anticipation of their marriage, now scheduled for May 1, 1978, they covenant:

1. *Separate properties.* Each possesses substantial separate properties, both real and personal. Each has advised the other of them and of significant indebtedness. Each is satisfied that a full and fair disclosure of property interests has been made. Their separate properties will remain separate throughout their marriage. Separate bank accounts will be maintained to channel separate funds, and separate books of account will be kept. They will arrange for a joint "operating" or "household" account with rights of survivorship as a convenience in paying for living and related expenses.

Without negating the expectation that they will consult together in respect to business affairs, Ann and James each retain the management and control of his or her separate property, whether real or personal, and each may encumber, sell, or dispose of such property without the consent of the other, unless the law of the applicable jurisdiction otherwise requires.

2. *Earnings after marriage.* As administrative assistant to the president of the ABCD Company, Ann is paid a substantial salary. Because Ann and James plan to move to a much smaller community than Evanston, the marriage will require her to withdraw from her present position, and it is unlikely that she would ever be able to secure an equivalent salary or even challenging employment. Ann has some income from investments, but her principal holdings are in a company which faces relatively large capital

outlays, and there is little likelihood that dividends will be paid in the foreseeable future. Real estate taxes on waterfront recreational property and her other obligations are such that most of her reduced future personal income will be consumed in meeting them, leaving her little more than "pin money" for herself.

Hence James recognizes that after the marriage, the maintenance of the new family will be his burden, and he would not wish it otherwise.

3. *Upon death of either party.* James is aware that Ann's separate holdings stem from the estate of her deceased husband. She feels that upon her death, properties which she has thus inherited (in sharp contrast to earned accumulations after her coming marriage to James and assets, if any, which she hereafter acquires from other sources) should descend to the children of her deceased husband and their issue. James is in sympathy with this viewpoint and will not assert whatever rights as husband he might otherwise acquire in such separate property of Ann, whether under the law of the state of Illinois or of Maine or of any state in which they may reside.

In his will or by life insurance, James will make suitable provisions for his wife, bearing in mind that, in all probability, upon his death, she would be unable to arrange for employment comparable to that which she is relinquishing in order to enter into their marriage. He will want her to be able to live in comfort and dignity in accordance with the standards customary to his family.

Ann does not wish to spell out any precise formula or dollar amount in respect to what provisions should be made for her in the will of James. Confident that they will live together in love and harmony and that he will be fair with her in respect to things financial (as well as in all matters), Ann leaves it to James to make whatever provision for her he deems just. She recognizes that after her death, properties which he has put in trust or otherwise earmarked to provide for her should pass to his children and their issue. Assuming provision is made for her consistent with the formula of the preceding paragraph, Ann relinquishes whatever dower or statutory rights she may have in the estate of James after his death.

4. *Further instruments.* At the request of the other, each party will execute and deliver whatever documents are found necessary or convenient to the accomplishment of the purposes of this agreement.

5. *Independent legal advice.* Each party has received the advice of independent counsel incident to the preparation and execution hereof.

6. *Successors bound.* This agreement is binding on the heirs, legatees, devisees, personal representatives, and other successors of each of the parties hereto.

7. *Effective date.* This agreement is effective as of the date of the marriage of the parties, whether it be in May 1978 as now planned or at some other date. Prior to marriage, each party will execute a will or codicil implementing this their plan and will always have in effect a testamentary document adequate for the accomplishment of their purposes, here recorded. If, unexpectedly, the marriage should not occur within one year, this contract shall terminate unless revived.

EXECUTED by both parties on January 15, 1978.

Ann A. Smith

James B. Howell

A prenuptial agreement must be signed before witnesses or acknowledged before a notary public as required by the state wherein it is executed or the couple may reside.

A checklist for prenuptial agreements

Here follows with briefest comment a listing of items which, when applicable, should be considered for inclusion in a prenuptial agreement.

1. *Identification and Use of Names.* Let there be no am-

biguities in respect to names. Initials only are scarcely suitable for a premarital contract. If a *nom de plume* has been customary, it may be used if one wishes, if preceded by the full legal name followed by "also known as"—whatever it may be.

The proper identification need not be supplemented by stilted phrases such as "first party" and "second party," then used artificially throughout the contract. Refer naturally to "Vivian" and "Harvey." If the bride is to continue to use her professional or business name, it is well to say so.

2. *Residence.* Include each of their present residences in the opening recitals. Sometimes a vague understanding to move to a new locality (northern Alaska!) should be made certain.

In stating residence, the fact that women are being elected more frequently to public offices should not be overlooked. Each public official must maintain her legal residence in the area whence she was elected. Should she marry a congressman from another state, the prenuptial agreement (which prudently they make public so that all their constituents may know) might well recite:

   a. The state, county, and city of his permanent and voting residence.

   b. Parallel data as to the politician bride.

   c. Their new joint transitory lodgings in Washington, D.C.

This principle may apply between counties or districts within the same state.

3. *Consideration.* Consideration is the motive, the price, the compelling influence which induces a contracting party to enter into a contract. It is silly to recite the consideration as "the sum of One Dollar in hand paid by first party to second party, receipt whereof hereby acknowledged." Yet respectable form books prepared to minimize thinking by lawyers contain such recitals. The mutual promises constitute the consideration.

4. *Target Date for Wedding.* There need be no

"whereas," or other artificial word, here or elsewhere in the contract, to dilute the flavor of a stipulation between lovers. Simply say that they plan to be married on or about a certain date and that this contract takes effect upon the completion of the marriage ceremony.

5. *Escape Clause.* If the wedding day is scheduled for many months ahead, the cautious may wish to include an escape clause to the effect that if the marriage ceremony is not performed within, say, a year, the agreement terminates and is of no legal effect. It can easily be resurrected, and perhaps modified, if nuptial plans are revived.

6. *His Assets and Liabilities.* What he owns and owes may be important, whether Vivian and Harvey have but little or one (or both) has much. What, if anything, should here be said will depend upon the circumstances of each couple. Sometimes there seems no need to catalog assets and liabilities; a general reference may be made as in the first paragraph of the prenuptial agreement on page 27. In other rare situations, financial statements should be appended to the contract.

7. *Her Assets and Liabilities.* The comments of paragraph 6 of the checklist apply. If either has substantial assets, the advantages and disadvantages of keeping properties separate or commingling, and how to do so, should be discussed with counsel. It might be appropriate to buy the family home with her funds and put it in her name, as her separate property. Paragraph 13 reminds you of taxes.

8. *Income from Investments and from Earnings.* There may be earned (salary; wages) income from the efforts of one or both. Or there may be no earned income. If income from investments and pensions is ample, some people may choose not to work. If there is no earned income in a community-property state, no community property will be accumulated. If the bride does not have a substantial separate estate, she should be protected financially by a contract. In any state, it may be planned that the bride work for a few years (until the

first baby comes) and that her earnings be earmarked as her separate savings. There is a wide range of possibilities.

9. *Household Expenses: Children.* Under varying circumstances it may be well for Vivian and Harvey to agree upon a formula for division of the new family budget. Perhaps both work; should they pool all income and expenses? Perhaps Vivian has two children by a former marriage and receives limited support money from a divorced husband. Should Harvey's savings be diverted to another man's children to put them through college? He hopes for a son of his own. Or suppose Vivian is of a wealthy family and enjoys an allowance from Aunt Ida as well as from her own devoted parents. She is accustomed to expensive attire. Should hardworking Harvey be expected to pay for all of it? There are many situations where an advance determination in respect to the allocation of financial burdens may be worth discussion and where the decision should be in writing.

10. *Vocational.* What if both have careers? She has an excellent post with a corporation and is expected to reach the top echelon. He is a successful interior decorator. Both live in Denver. She is subject to transfer; a fair prognosis is three more transfers before becoming a vice-president with headquarters in New York. Should Harvey agree in advance to sell his shop, leave his loyal clients, and follow Vivian to the ends of the earth? Or should Vivian seek another job in Denver?

11. *Division of Property in the Event of Separation.* It can be charged that reference to a possible separation in the prenuptial agreement is an anachronism. Romantically that is true; it is morbid to mention the possibility of disaster. But, practically, in occasional situations, the property aspect of a possible separation should not be ignored.

Suppose by inheritance the bride-to-be is wealthy or, upon a death or two, will be. Or assume her to be a jazz singer and a fabulous earner. She enjoys the benefits of a shrewd agent;

a considerable fortune has already been amassed. She is fond of a delightful playboy whose marriage record is no better than his sporadic attempts at composing movie scripts. Would it not be prudent for her to include a "payoff" formula in their first agreement?

Or, defying the pleadings of his parents, aunts, and uncles, the scion of a wealthy family insists on marrying the divorcée whom he met on the 727 en route to Rio. Should not the ever pessimistic lawyer try to arrange a buy-out price in a property settlement agreement?

These are not frequent situations, but neither are they atypical. When there is a rational fear (I did not quite say "expectation") of a separation, advance planning may not be amiss. Provisions of this sort are inherently "iffy." What if they have children and nevertheless decide to part? The formulas reached in advance may be completely outmoded.

In a sense, it is repetitious to remind you that in this item 11, the word "separation" has been used, not "divorce" or "dissolution." Courts have held that an agreement to divorce or one which encourages or facilitates a divorce is unenforceable. We start from the ancient doctrine that divorces could be decreed only by the ecclesiastical courts. Now, of course, in the United States, jurisdiction is in the civil courts. Termination of the marriage contract (see "The Marriage Contract") must be approved by the state through its instrument, the judicial system. Not even under the currently fashionable philosophy of no-fault dissolution proceedings do the unhappy marrieds enjoy the prerogative of untangling themselves without the seal of governmental approval. Society is interested in marriage as a *status*, which is beyond a commercial contract.

Your attorney will know the limitations upon references to divisions of property in the event of separation which prevail in your jurisdiction.

12. *Death; Wills.* While unpleasant to discuss, division

of property in the event of death does not carry the odium of item 11. When there are disparities in respect to age and wealth—say, a rich wife and penniless husband—assurance in respect to the minimum provisions of a will may be in order. Each is obligated to keep in effect a will consistent with their agreement.

13. *Taxes.* This paragraph will be of interest only to the favored few who possess substantial wealth. Judicious planning in advance of marriage may cut down the impact of taxes. If astute, the prospective opulent bride and groom will consult with counsel and tax advisers.

14. *Other Documents.* There should be included the conventional paragraph reciting that Vivian and Harvey will execute further documents as may be found necessary or convenient in the performance of the prenuptial agreement.

15. *Competency to Contract.* The age at which a girl may marry may be younger than that of a boy. Sixteen against eighteen, for example, or eighteen against twenty-one. Requirements vary from state to state and are subject to legislative changes. If a prenuptial contract is envisaged by the young couple, date of birth should be told the lawyer even though he does not ask it. He probably will—during the first few minutes of the first interview. The application for the marriage license will include the same question. In some states, parental consent will be required below a given age.

16. *Separate Counsel.* It is perhaps natural for Vivian and Harvey to go to one or the other's attorney, or to one they both know, to draw or review the prenuptial agreement. But another attorney should be retained to scrutinize it from the standpoint of the other party. Counsel should not purport to act for both. Years later a lawyer may be accused of favoring one against the other, whether in the wording of the contract or in assisting the primary client in being less than frank in respect to property matters.

17. *Adoptable Children.* Should there be an agreement to

adopt if there are adoptable children from a former marriage, or an illegitimate child of the never-wed bride-to-be? Not infrequently children of a divorced person are not adoptable—at least not without litigation—because of the refusal of the other natural parent to give consent.

The right of adoption was unknown to the common law of England. Hence, in almost all of our jurisdictions, prerequisites to and methods of adoption are purely statutory. The courts are strict in protecting the rights of the child's natural parents. States differ in statutory language. Fundamental to all is that the best interest of the child is paramount. Often when a divorced parent has *exclusive* custody, the consent of the other parent is not required.

Even if there are no legal obstacles, it may be prudent to defer adoptions for a time sufficient to feel sure that the new marriage is for life.

Consistent with the fiduciary duty of frankness reviewed in the section entitled "The Betrothal," if the prospective bride believes she cannot bear children (or the groom beget), this should be discussed, perhaps ending with a plan to adopt. Later, of course, they may surprise themselves by having children of their own.

18. *What Law Governs.*   There are now fifty states. We are a mobile people; not a few are industrialized gypsies. When the prospective bride and groom are residents of the same state, their lawyers will probably agree that the laws of that state will govern the contract. If from different states, there might be a choice—perhaps one state is better than the other for both of them.

Or they might both be temporarily in a third state or abroad. The possible desirability of predetermining jurisdiction should not be forgotten.

19. *Arbitration.*   Perhaps both attorneys and the principals opt for an arbitration agreement. There are many variations in formula, far too many to discuss here. A covenant to

arbitrate should not be included unless everyone feels a positive "yes," both as to terms and method of choosing the arbiters.

There is one glaring deliberate omission from the foregoing checklist. It may be too delicate—too intimate—a matter for written contractual specifications, particularly by first-timers. And violations may always be said to have been unintended. It is the question of how many children shall they have—a question different from adoption.

The ultraserious-minded bride or bridegroom may think the population explosion must be quickly ended. Otherwise, the person argues, the pressure for food and space will make an atomic Armageddon inevitable.

But this person's happy, optimistic spouse-to-be, an only child, wants a big family. What fun they would have! The thought of the cost of shoes for children in an inflationary economy does not come to mind.

Here we face a fundamental of the marriage relationship. No children? One or two? A big brood—presumably all well, happy, and bright? Their advance decision, if they have one, will seldom be found in a written prenuptial contract. Yet to march blithely down the aisle with the most important of all questions left unanswered, perhaps scarcely discussed, does not reflect sagacious agreement in respect to an essential of a felicitous marriage.

It is my impression that more and more young people are facing up to the realities of family planning. But I have not listed this most important of all family programs among the paragraphs to be written and signed. For some couples, perhaps it should be; it is for them to decide.

Day-to-day details

There is another species of prenuptial contract. It is adaptable to subsequent as well as to first marriages.

Occasionally magazines and Sunday supplements print the texts of detailed prenuptial operating programs. They spell out household duties with great care—cooking, dishwashing, cleaning, care of pets, dusting, and laundry. They cover budgets, a partner's freedom (or lack of it) to be away weekends for hunting and fishing, and their annual vacations. One pair signed up for separate holidays so that each might have leisure to "meditate and restore personality"—a somewhat vague objective.

One foresighted woman wrote into their plan that twenty times a year, on an evening of her choice, he would forgo TV sports, dress up, and escort her to a cultural event selected by her, no matter how bored he might be.

There was a "no children" provision, permitting each spouse to pursue a career unhampered by diapers and measles. Another agreement took a long look ahead and segregated responsibilities in respect to the rearing of offspring.

One prudent couple covered the dilemma of cats. She loved them and had two or three. He had an allergy to animal dander. She gave in, and he promised her pedigreed canaries.

In today's complicated environment, detailed written operating plans for marital life may have considerable merit. At very least, they require the bewildered explorers to try to think things through. As long as she has an outside job or career, he ought to help with the housework—not spasmodically but regularly, and be willing to pledge himself to do so.

But to be feasible past the first anniversary, it is likely that both must have a sense of humor and be pliable—willing to modify details of an agreement made under artificial circumstances between people inexperienced in marriage, at least with each other. I favor written operational specifications for those who crave them if, but only if, both parties realize that dogmatic details are transitory, perhaps a valuable lubricant during the adjustment period, but not chiseled in granite to endure for life.

If either spouse is adamant and brittle in respect to minutiae, forever pointing to a phrase in their detailed prenuptial declaration of operating procedures, dire troubles lie ahead.

As conditions change, and most certainly they will, the written parchment will become as obsolete as an ox-drawn plow in the Iowa corn belt. In typical families, for many years the document will be mislaid with old letters and mementos in a trunk in the attic. With good luck, it may be found by grandmother in time to be read aloud at the fiftieth-anniversary dinner. Having observed the realities of the division of family affairs, the children and grandchildren will deem it hilarious. There will be demand for Xerox copies.

These personalized self-made operational schemes may seem less than legal, not justifying the bother and expense of a visit to a lawyer's office. Yet I venture to suggest that the document should be scrutinized by counsel. It may contain binding commitments, the meaning and significance of which were not understood by both.

Religious predilections; personal conduct

There is another important aspect of life regarding which there should be premarital agreements, at least in principle. But perhaps a reduction to writing would appear unseemly to many couples. (Between regal families, it might be inscribed on parchment and signed and sealed as a treaty!) The question is: In what religion shall the children be reared? Many couples have no fervent religious bias, or one of them is willing to accede to the other's preference so far as the children are concerned. This Sunday school, or that Sunday school, or none at all. In such a framework, there is no religious problem when deciding where to christen or baptize. The next two paragraphs do not apply to couples taking that neutral stance.

Janet, born and schooled in the Scottish Highlands, is as Presbyterian as was John Knox. Her fiancé Patrick is as Roman Catholic as was Bishop Ussher. They had better agree on the religious environment for their children before the organist turns to *Lohengrin*. If Patrick or his parents insist on a marriage in the Catholic Church, the lovers may be forced to make á pledge in this regard.

But disregarding the persuasions of priest and preacher, even the Janets and Patricks of lesser religious intensity should reach an agreement between each other in respect to churchly environment. Afterward, of course, they may change their minds and send the children to the community interdenominational church.

Where they (Janet and Patrick) should themselves attend church—if either or both do—is much easier. Patrick can go to early mass and return home in time to help Janet with breakfast and the weekly ordeal of putting the children in their Sunday best. Or the adults may go to any church or synagogue together; alternate; or not attend Divine Worship. The important aspect is what religious environment will surround the children.

Now and then the press and newscasts tell of a remarriage within the jet set which is predicated upon the recurrent partner giving up dope, or cutting down on demon rum, or abjuring some other vice. It would not be surprising if, occasionally, the bride or bridegroom insisted that these promises be put in writing.

Covenants of this sort cannot be enforced as can be a solid stipulation to pay a sum of money or to convey a parcel of land. But they are not without value. If skillfully worded, they reduce to certainty oral promises which may be equivocal; an oral "I intend to" is not the equivalent of a written "I will."

There is a tendency to live up to a written promise—or at least to make a real effort to do so—when one might shrug off an oral commitment as mere conversation, the specifics of which had long since been forgotten. Since cuneiform inscriptions were first scratched on Persian cliffs, the written word has had a coercive value.

A prospective spouse who, with friends, has been experimenting with heroin might stand firm in following a written pledge to abjure the drug, while an oral declaration would be short-lived.

Hence it is suggested that in certain acute, scattered situations, specific written promises covering conduct may be constructive. Sybil wants to marry Oliver, but not unless she feels sure he will discontinue one or two identifiable activities. The older generation tells her she should not marry a man to reform him; she must take him as he is or not at all. Her reply is that she has no intention of trying to transform him; she loves him well enough as is. But she simply cannot tolerate excessive drinking, or whatever the problem may be.

If Oliver truly means to live up to the promises he made before the fireplace, he should be willing to put them on paper, above his signature. If he is unwilling to be so definite, if Oliver insists on vagueness, this is a good time for Sybil to face the facts of life.

It has not been suggested that Sybil should count on legal enforcement of such a pledge, although it might turn out to be legally advantageous. If marital disaster should come, a bitter court battle might ensue. The judge could well look with disfavor upon a man who persistently violated pledges clearly spelled out as an inducement to marriage.

But, of course, a negative or punitive use of Oliver's covenants should not be in Sybil's mind as she plans for their wedding. She should be relying in good faith upon the promise that as a gentleman Oliver will make good.

In some cases, confronting a promise of personal conduct can prevent a disastrous marriage. For example, I knew a young man who smoked moderately; he broke his engagement to a delightful woman because she would not promise to give up chain smoking. The doctor said it would be impossible for her to cut down to three or four cigarettes a day. It would be necessary for her to abandon all smoking. She tried total abstinence for a few weeks and then decided that for her the fags were more important than the fellow. Frankly facing the requirement of definite contractual promises probably saved the torture of an unsound marriage.

There is a unique relationship where, if possible, there should *not* be a prenuptial agreement, but, instead, a record sufficient to show that there was no betrothal. These are the situations where an affluent, lonely oldster is under the dominance of a nurse-housekeeper. Likely it is an old man, a widower, being cared for by a twice- or thrice-married, middle-aged nurse. A simple employment contract can negative a claim of a promise to marry. The employment contract may provide for a bonus to be paid if she stands by until the end—perhaps in part based on length of service. The longer he lives, the bigger the bonus; an incentive to kindly care!

Many readers will have heard of instances where he married the nurse. The venerable bridegroom made a new will leaving a token to his neglectful children who rallied around only when informed he was on his deathbed.

In most jurisdictions, if he does *not* make a new will or add a codicil providing for his bride, he will have died intestate (without a will) so far as she is concerned. This may place her ahead of the children as to receiving a major portion, or even all, of his property, depending on the law of that state. It invites litigation.

If wise, or rightly advised, before he marries the nurse, he will have made a prenuptial agreement spelling out what she is to receive at the time of his passing, a generous amount if she is faithful and nurses him until death. A lesser amount if she should leave him.

As a consideration to the one who makes the will, in the prenuptial agreement the nurse should relinquish all other claims against or interests in the estate.

If an aged widow should be duped into marrying a male nurse, similar admonitions would apply.

However, a better route for the ailing would usually be to

foreclose the idea of marriage by an employment contract enduring until death. Of course, no matter how ill the patient is today, the nurse might go first, ending whatever contract has been made.

An agreement *not* to marry is usually unenforceable and is not indicated in this situation. An affirmative, fairly balanced, written commitment to stand by as long as the patient lives is a contradiction of a claim by the nurse that he had promised to marry her, or she him. If the loyalty of the nurse is to be assured by contract, it must be generous in relation to the resources of the patient. It might be three-pronged: (1) going salary for permanent practical nurses, *plus* (2) a modest annual or semiannual bonus, *plus* (3) a bequest in the patient's will if the nurse is able to and does well perform a nurse's duties until the passing.

The essence then is that the musts are (1) if a marriage is to take place, the execution of a written prenuptial contract and a consistent will limiting the new spouse to a realistic amount when the elderly patient dies, *or* (2) a written employment agreement which makes equitable provision for the nurse and thus negates a false claim that there was either an oral betrothal contract or a promise of a lavish bequest.

A retired industrialist well into his eighties lived in suburban New York and Florida. Long a widower, he had an attractive, competent, and diligent nurse. She supervised the cook and gardener and attended to various household matters, in addition to being an excellent attendant at the sick bed.

The only son, not very well situated financially, resided in Oregon. He was delighted that his father had such satisfactory arrangements. His wife sent Christmas cards to the father, and once in a long time a letter, telling of the grandchildren. But they seldom visited; three years had elapsed since last they saw him. They did not even know about it when some eighteen months before death, he married the nurse. They learned of it when he died, leaving them a pittance and the rest of the huge estate to the new wife.

This is an extreme case in terms of the amount of money involved—not a dollar earmarked to help with the education of the grandchildren. The point of the illustration is that it behooves children and in due course grandchildren to maintain close ties with the aged and try to see to it that there is a proper contract if there is a permanent nursing relationship which might lead to marriage or a promise of it.

From the standpoint of the nurse, relationships with the patient should not be such that the will may be subject to plausible contest on the ground of undue influence. It should be prepared by the patient's own lawyer. The witnesses should be people who would be persuasive if the maker's competency to execute a will were challenged in court. The nurse should not be in the room during the signing ceremony.

A reminder

Any widow who enjoys pension, Social Security, or other benefits stemming from the death of her husband should check with her attorney as to the possible impact of remarriage.

3

The Marriage Contract

The wedding is thought of as a ceremony ranging in formality from a simple procedure in the office of a justice of the peace to a ritual with eight bridesmaids and a ring-bearer marching down the long aisle of a cathedral. The formalities, the pretty dresses, the flowers, and the wedding reception which follow are but the wrappings for a contract, partly oral and partly written, when the functionary and the bride and groom sign whatever paper is prescribed by the law of the place where the wedding ceremony is performed. Either ceremony constitutes a marriage.

In ancient times, marriages by proxy were not unknown; those solemnized by long-distance telephone of course came after Alexander Graham Bell. Imagine a marine away at the wars. A letter from his sweetheart reminds him of their trip to the resort hotel during his last leave; as a result, she is pregnant. He wants to marry her; another immediate leave was refused. Since he cannot be home for the wedding, he appoints his brother to stand in his stead, as his proxy. A number of states recognize a proxy marriage as valid when it is literally impossible for the bride and groom to be together. The child will be legitimate, and mother and child will be entitled to the financial benefits received by the family of a fighting man.

There are instances where marriage vows are made by telephone—a conference-call type of hookup. The bride on one line, the groom on another, and the minister or officiating officer (perhaps a judge) on the third.

But it must be remembered that, in many states, the statutory requirements for a valid marriage are such that neither a bride nor groom may be represented vicariously. For example, they may be required to appear together, in person, when applying for a marriage license, then follow medical examinations and a designated wait-and-see period. No one should risk a proxy or long-distance ceremony without approval of local counsel, competent in this segment of the law. A wedding on TV might be quite different. In the eyes of most viewers, it would be in bad taste. But all essential parties could be on the stage at once. Some churches including, I am told, the Roman Catholic, recognize marriage by proxy, but have not yet accepted the telephonic variation.

Nature of the contract

Following the language of a federal court, the rights and duties of husband and wife in the marriage relationship spring from the marriage contract. These rights and duties are mutual and coextensive in character. Husband and wife are entitled to equal protection under the law.

Time was when this could not have been said under our law and, of course, cannot yet be said in some civilizations. Anglo-American legal evolution on this subject began with a theory under which, by marriage, the husband and wife became one person, and he was it. The legal existence of the woman was merged within that of the husband. Marriage extinguished contractual indebtedness between the parties; a few states still so hold.

Soon, we hope, the subservient position of woman will everywhere be a thing of the past. Under the statutory Married Women's Acts found in many states, other legislative relief, and the community-property concept which controls in eight states,* women have been accorded a parity beyond the dreams of the British Pankhursts, mother and daughters, and other pioneers in women's liberation movements. So far have the legal rights of women advanced, and so fast have the legal disabilities of married women been wiped out, that in commenting on a recent proposed initiative measure touted as making women "equal to men" an intelligent, hardworking young matron could say: "Why should I vote for equality with men? I am already superior."

As we review the rights and obligations of husband and wife deriving from the marriage contract, we see citizens legally

---

* Arizona, California, Idaho, Louisiana, Nevada, New Mexico, Texas, and Washington.

equal under the law of the land, subject only to an occasional vestigial oddity.

The marriage contract is unique; it differs from all other contracts. It confers a status; it creates a family unit which most people deem vital to the continuity of civilization.

It is so important that (a handful of countries still to the contrary) it cannot be abrogated without following prescribed procedures.

In contrast, the parties to commercial compacts can almost always terminate (rescind) their agreement whenever they choose to do so, unless they are adversely affecting the rights of third parties who are legally entitled to rely on the contract in question, have done so, and would be injured by its conclusion.

Inherent rights and duties

In the section "Agreements during Marriage" we will survey types of contracts between husband and wife—business partnerships, investments and loans, ownerships, and others—which are not inherently *within* the marriage vows. Here, with briefest comment, we will look at the contractual obligations which exist the moment a man and a woman are pronounced husband and wife.

As is its habit, the law has evolved a cabalistic word to apply to these reciprocal obligations; it is "consortium." That word may be defined to include companionship; cooperative attainment of felicity; comfort and mutual aid during periods of sickness and distress; collaboration in sex and all other things expectable within a loyal family. They should follow from affection; but they are also legal obligations which, one may well say, are unenforceable by any court if affection has withered. But failure to perform is a violation of a legal duty which may have a legal impact if there should be litigation between the parties to the marital contract.

Consortium traditionally includes the wife's right to support by the husband. He must provide her with a home, the necessities of life, and amenities within his means. During recent years, this right has, in millions of families, become outmoded by changing economic conditions and widespread participation by women in the work force. That both would stay on payrolls, for a time at least, is often implicit in the betrothal contract or recited in a prenuptial agreement. So it can no longer be assumed with confidence that the new husband has impliedly agreed that the full support of the family shall be on his shoulders alone.

Consortium includes the performance by the wife of age-old household and domestic duties and care of children—perhaps sharply modified by her new status as herself an earner, whose stipend may equal or excel that of her husband. In such a situation, as an aspect of consortium, does not the husband assume a reciprocal duty of helping with household routines? It is obviously impossible to talk in terms of dollars and percentages. Relative health may be a factor. A changed economy and way of life have modified the ancient simple division of labor contemplated by consortium.

Nevertheless, the basic rule remains that consortium comprehends performance by a wife of household and domestic duties according to the couple's economic and social station in life, all without monetary or equivalent compensation. As a matter of fact, myriad hardworking, floor-polishing wives are "paid" at a lower rate than a day housecleaner. They usually average less in dollars from the family budget for their clothes and to spend as they choose than do other toilers in the economic community. Yet a contract to pay a housewife in money for the performance of these services is void for want of consideration! By virtue of the marriage contract, she is already contractually bound to perform them.

Assume a family lives upon and operates one of the vanishing family farms. As part of her "household" duties, she gleans a cash crop from her chickens and vegetable garden. Until the recent development of intricate farm machinery and specialized raising of fowls and growing of vegetables, I suppose that helping on the farm was an aspect of consortium. Shifting from country to city, there may be parallel situations.

If, prior to the betrothal, the man or woman operated a "mom-and-pop" business—a delicatessen, a dry-cleaning establishment, a novelty shop—I suppose that helping in the family business might classify as a phase of consortium. However, the answer should be otherwise if, against her wishes, the husband insists that he save a bookkeeper's salary he can well afford to pay by drafting his wife as an unpaid bookkeeper. That, I think, would not be classed as consortium. A promise to pay her a salary would be enforceable.

This contractual right of consortium which comes into being with the marriage vows has a value which, even outside a divorce court, can be measured in dollars. More than a score of states have held that when someone has negligently injured another person's husband, the wife has a cause of action and may recover damages. Illustrating the difficulty in determining sound social policy in legal principles primarily concerned with persons, about the same number of states still deny her recovery. But these decisions do not dilute the duties in respect to consortium as between husband and wife.

A leading case on the subject arose in federal court. Refusing to follow the "medieval concept"—the judge called it—of the marriage relationship denying the wife the right of recovery for injuries to her husband, the court reasoned that husband and wife have equal rights in the marriage contract and are entitled to equal protection under the law.

A New York judge faced the argument that loss of consortium is essentially an emotional loss (in contrast to loss of support) and not subject to valuation. He decided against the defendant elevator company which urged that the rights known as consortium are too personal, too intangible and conjectural, to be measured in pecuniary terms by a jury. The court recognized that consortium represents the interest of the injured party's spouse in the continuance of a healthy and happy marital life which embraces elements such as love, companionship, affection, society, sexual relations, solace, and more—all personal but, the judge ruled, very real, and the hurt from losing them can be assuaged by a monetary award.

Thus it is a fundamental of Anglo-American jurisprudence that the relationship of husband and wife imposes on each of them varied marital duties and also accords to each legal marital rights beyond those pertaining to property and business affairs. Once married, special contracts concerning these inherent obligations are usually held ineffective because of lack of an additional consideration—meaning something of value which is an incentive to the other party to enter into the contract. If John is already legally obligated to pay Joseph 100 guilders, what benefit (consideration) does Joseph receive from a second, a duplicate, promise to pay the same guilders?

So it is with a repetition by one spouse of commitments intrinsic to the marriage vows. It is merely a *re*-promise to do something already legally, and often sacredly, promised. The courts have frequently held such a replica to be insufficient consideration to support a commitment by the other spouse to do something extra (deed the farm to the wife's son by a prior marriage) which he was *not* legally obligated to do. That would be demanding something for nothing.

Termination of contract

In many civilizations, a husband could (and in a few, still can) terminate the marriage contract by telling his wife to go; no ritual was required. Slightly more strict, the Arabs did prescribe a formula. The word *ittalch* (literally, "go to the devil") must be repeated three times by the discontented husband. Arab wives did not enjoy reciprocal power of termination. But in other civilizations they did; in some they still do.

After Justinian, Roman wives did. Roman law held that both marriage and divorce were private affairs between the contracting parties. The departing spouse had to send a letter to the other terminating the marriage and releasing any interest in the other's property. The courts intervened only when the spouses could not compose their differences regarding property rights or care or custody of children.

In Old Testament days, the right of divorce was taken for granted. The law prescribed a Bill of Divorcement. The wife was entitled to a paper showing her new freedom. An ancient form recited: "Up to this moment you have been my wife. But now you are released and set free so that you may be your own mistress and marry whomever you desire. You have received from me (the husband) a Bill of Freedom, according to the Law of Moses and Israel." The New Testament is not so liberal. It certainly frowns on divorce except on the grounds of adultery. Some pious people deem it completely forbidden.

In sharp contrast to the Roman tradition and to primitive peoples, Anglo-Saxon law has long required some grounds for divorce, and American divorce law is based on the premise that the state is interested in the marital status and that (except in Hollywood) husbands and wives are not discardable and interchangeable.

The term, the duration, of the usual American marriage contract is "until death do us part." But now that is being intoned tongue in cheek. This must be particularly so in those states which have adopted a so-called no-fault divorce law, which in essence provides for the dissolution of a marriage upon a finding that the marriage is no longer viable. If the husband and wife agree that it is not, that pretty well proves it, subject to the qualification, later elaborated, that the court is not bound to follow their wishes, though it usually does. If they have entered into a property-settlement agreement (see "Property Settlement and Separation Agreements"), there may be nothing difficult for the divorce court to decide unless minor children are involved. Then, when itself determining or ratifying the parents' provisions concerning custody and support, the court may probe the conduct of the parties. The welfare of the children is paramount. Hence the conduct of each parent, a way of saying "relative blame" of each, may become important. And, as will be seen shortly, conduct may be considered important by a judge who must decide whether or not a reconciliation should be attempted, despite what the spouses say. This is in furtherance of public policy; the law is concerned about the preservation of the family, a basic unit of society. It may not be legally dissolved without permission of the sovereign state, communicated through the courts.

In an increasing number of states, proceedings to terminate a marriage contract are no longer called "divorce." In the courthouse files, they are no longer entitled "Mary Smith versus John Smith." The new terminology is "In re Smith dissolution," or a similar denomination, which does not connote an *adversary* proceeding as does "Smith versus Smith." All this is quite new in America. It is not yet universal among the half hundred jurisdictions within the United States and may never be.

Formerly in this country, divorce was granted only upon a showing of fault. Each state has had an opportunity to enact and amend its own divorce laws; they differ widely. Since before the Ten Commandments, adultery has been considered the most serious of all marital offenses. In the past, in some of our states it was the only ground for divorce. Variously worded, state by state, other grounds have included: commission and conviction of a serious crime; fraud, as defined by the particular divorce statute and interpreted by the supreme court of that state; impotency, habitual drunkenness, or use of narcotics; desertion; and the omnibus less obnoxious allegation that the defendant has been guilty of physical or mental cruelty, making life burdensome and the continuance of the marital relationship impossible. Insanity is a good reason for divorce; if unknown to the innocent party at the time of the wedding, incurable insanity may make the marriage void *ad initio*—from the beginning. Then there might be an annulment rather than a divorce.

There are no common-law (law by court decision) grounds

for divorce. They are as prescribed by statute; each legislature is omnipotent. State supreme courts have held that a legislature has authority to enact divorce statutes which make a distinction between the causes for which a divorce will be granted to a husband and those which entitle a wife to an equivalent decree. In the present judicial climate, it is expectable that, if a divorce statute which discriminates on the basis of sex should be before the Supreme Court of the United States, it would be struck down as in violation of the Constitution.

Passing mention was made of annulment in contrast to divorce, or now, dissolution. It is the other legal device by which the law terminates a marriage contract before the termination date as agreed upon by the parties during the marriage ritual—death. Actions for separate maintenance differ sharply from those asking for divorce or annulment. A plea for separate maintenance affirms the marriage contract and prays that the defendant be required to perform properly.

Grounds for annulment may overlap the statutory grounds for divorce. Thus legislatures frequently specify insanity, fraud, or impotency as grounds for divorce although, in that very jurisdiction (state), each may also constitute an adequate reason for annulment. Annulment, also subject to legislative mandates but not wholly dependent upon them, may frequently be predicated upon: an undissolved prior marriage; violation of a prior divorce decree or a statute barring remarriage; marriage entered into with the intention that it should not be binding; a mock or trial marriage; the fact that one of the participants was under the age of consent; an incestuous marriage; duress; concealment of a loathsome disease such as syphilis; misrepresentation in regard to chastity or prenuptial pregnancy as well as the three causes (insanity, fraud, and impotency) previously mentioned.

What constitutes incest varies greatly state by state. Lineal consanguinity is universally forbidden. But in one state the ban may begin with marriages between first cousins and another with second.

The fundamental distinction between an annulment and a divorce or dissolution proceeding is that the latter is instituted to sever a marriage relation admitted to exist, whereas an annulment proceeding is for the purpose of securing a judicial decree that because of some impediment existing at the moment of the marriage ceremony, no valid marriage contract was made. Another way of saying it is: Usually an annulment proceeding is based on reasons which existed at the time of the marriage; in contrast, a divorce or dissolution is for causes arising after the marriage, perhaps after many years of happy marriage.

A child is born during a marriage which is later annulled. In legal contemplation, there never was a valid marriage. Yet the child is legitimate and remains so after the court decree is entered declaring the "marriage" invalid—nonexistent. The rule should apply to a child conceived during the span of the false marriage though born after the annulment.

Since we must recognize, if not joyfully ride, the wave of the future, let us return to no-fault divorce statutes. There is an admirable organization called the National Conference of Commissioners on Uniform State Laws. After careful and usually prolonged research and study, it drafts and recommends statutes for adoption by state legislatures. In 1971 it came forth with a Uniform Divorce Act, which has been approved as to the no-fault aspect by the Family Law Section of the American Bar Association. It zeros in on one ground for divorce: "Irretrievable breakdown of marriage." Some state legislatures have already adopted that language. Others prefer "irreconcilable differences" or "irretrievably broken." Instead of exploiting the delinquencies of the defendant spouse, all that the husband or wife who seeks a divorce need allege to show grounds is that there has been an irretrievable breakdown of the marriage relationship (or "irreconcilable differences have arisen," depending on the jurisdiction wherein the proceeding is brought) and there is no reasonable likelihood that the marriage can be preserved.

Oklahoma and Oregon, for example, stand next to each other in the list of states; otherwise there are notable disparities in background and culture. Yet both (in 1971 and 1972) embraced the no-fault divorce philosophy. Oklahoma opted for the "irretrievable-breakdown" approach and Oregon preferred an "irreconcilable-differences" formula. Already, or soon, court decisions in each state will make their laws variant. The only way to ascertain just what the law of your state is, as of time of reading, is to consult competent counsel. That is because the new statutory no-fault language is vague and uncertain. No guidelines are spelled out. What is an "irreconcilable difference"? Is the test subjective, in the mind of only one of the pair? What if the other spouse still believes reconciliation is possible? Or, if the state statute permits, the trial judge may view reconciliation as possible even though both parties think otherwise.

The no-fault divorce statutes have to do with grounds for dissolution; they do not establish a regime of divorce by mutual consent. I know of no state which has abdicated its authority in regard to marriage or said to the spouses, "Terminate your marriage agreement whenever you choose." Indeed, since the enactment of no-fault statutes, eminent courts have said the opposite. A widespread notion that under the no-fault theory a divorce is always available, if either spouse wants it, does not stand up.

To back my understanding, I will briefly review a few cases holding that the statutes do not authorize dissolution of the marriage contract on the whim of a spouse. The decisions are to the effect that dissolution should be decreed only when the court is of the opinion that the marriage has broken down to the extent that the legitimate ends of matrimony have been destroyed and no reasonable possibility of reconciliation exists.

After the adoption of its irreconcilable-differences statutes in 1969, there was rendered a California decision called *McKim* v. *McKim*. The appellate opinion stated that the legislature enacted a statute authorizing dissolution of marriage if there are irreconcilable differences between husband and wife which have resulted in an irremediable breakdown of the marriage. The legislators intended that so far as possible dissolution proceedings should be nonadversary. But, the legislature did *not* mandate that a dissolution of marriage could be obtained by consent alone. Nor did the legislature ordain that the trial judge should be perfunctory when determining that irreconcilable differences do exist.

Another California decision (it is the pioneer state in this field) abandons the "versus" and adopts the new terminology "Re Marriage of *Walton*." Sustaining the new dissolution of marriage statute from attack on the ground of unpermissible vagueness, and emphasizing that the possibility of reconciliation is the important issue, the court asserted that the law did not constitute a license for dissolution by the consent of the parties. The judges recognize that to a considerable extent the future of the marriage depends on the subjective state of mind of the couple. Nevertheless, they hold that, in the final analysis the court, not the parties, must decide whether the evidence adduced supports findings that irreconcilable differences do exist and that the marriage has broken down irremediably and should be dissolved.

Florida was two years behind California in adopting the new law. So a 1972 title, *Riley* versus *Riley*, still carries the adversary atmosphere. But the opinion of the appellate court did not. It rather favored the vagueness of the statute, the lack of guidelines. The trial judge is left free to decide each case on its merits. If uncertain as to whether the differences are irreconcilable, the judge should prescribe a trial period, say three months, within which to find out. In every case the important issue is the possibility of reconciliation. It is not a simple matter of a mate saying, "I want out." Before dissolution is granted, the trial court should be satisfied that the parties can no longer live together, because their difficulties are so deep and substantial that no reasonable effort could eradicate them so as to enable the parties to live together in a normal marital relationship.

An Oregon court also based its decision on the situation between the parties as *established by the evidence*. If the parties disagree, the proof of their irreconcilable differences may be as nasty as under the traditional reasons for divorce.

Iowa adopted an irretrievable-breakdown type statute in 1970, shortly after California, but a year before Oregon. In a case entitled in the new nonadversary style, Re Marriage of *Collins*, the petition of the wife for dissolution was resisted by a stubborn husband. In order to show the marriage was no longer viable, the wife introduced evidence to prove that the husband had forced the family to live in substandard housing, although they could afford better. Likewise to save money, he did not provide them with clothing and creature comforts commensurate with the family's financial position. He insisted that the wife and children follow his religious convictions, anathema to the wife. He physically abused the children as well as the petitioning wife. And he insisted on sexual practices abhorrent to her. All of this was to prove an irretrievable breakdown which had been denied by the husband.

If the parties have not made a separation agreement (see "Property Settlement and Separation Agreements"), or if the custody of children is in controversy, in some no-fault states the battle over property and children may be as venomous as under any of the traditional statutes. So it is that those who harbor the thought that the "progressive" enactments have made all divorce proceedings painless should reorient their thinking. Even though both parties want a dissolution, more may be required than the payment of a modest fee to a clerk at the county courthouse. Of course, in many if not most instances, the new statutes achieve their purpose. Divorce (dissolution) is a simpler and easier procedure than it was before their enactment.

The Women's Bureau of the U.S. Department of Labor prepared a chart showing that as of October 1, 1973, a type of no-fault divorce legislation has been adopted in twenty-two states.* Undoubtedly there have been some since then. It is impossible to be precise without quoting directly from the statutes and decisions of each state. A few may consider themselves in the no-fault classification merely because a divorce may be obtained without proving more than living apart for a designated period—the spread is one to five years. But living permanently apart has long been recognized in a significant number of jurisdictions. Whether a true no-fault concept will ever be embraced by all the states is problematical.

Termination resulting from alienation of affections deserves a few words. When discussing the legal effects of betrothal contracts (see "The Betrothal"), attention was given that subject. The rule applying to suits based on alienating the affections of a fiancé or fiancée apply with equal or greater vigor to alienating the affections of a spouse. Some courts even permit a child, a third-party beneficiary of the marriage contract, to bring suit and recover damages against a person who causes a parent to breach the marriage contract by neglecting his parental duties, as by desertion. If a rake runs away with a mother, in some states he may be required to pay damages to the children as well as to the deserted husband. In other states the law would award no recompense.

Under the catchy headline "Love's Litigation Lost," the Seattle *Post-Intelligencer* recently published an Associated Press dispatch telling of a liberal-minded trial judge who ruled that a woman is entitled to choose her sexual partner. He con-

* Alabama, Arizona, California, Colorado, Connecticut, Florida, Georgia, Hawaii, Idaho, Indiana, Iowa, Kentucky, Maine, Michigan, Montana, Nebraska, Nevada, New Hampshire, North Dakota, Oregon, Texas, and Washington.

siders that a legal principle which affords a husband damages predicated upon the sexual activity of the wife with another man is "abhorrent and repugnant to modern standards." The judge threw a sop to the orthodox, stressing that he was not favoring marital infidelity; he was merely acknowledging what he considered "to be a given fact in the evolution of our moral and sexual mores."

His Honor's mores certainly have evolved a long way from the cultures wherein the wayward wife and perhaps also her paramour would be subject to dire criminal sanctions—for example, locked in the pillory, exposed to public derision.

Very occasionally a third party must pay the fiddler when a marriage contract is terminated by divorce. A loyal brother wanted XYZ to marry his sister. As an inducement to XYZ to do so, the brother promised to indemnify him for any money he might pay for the support of his wife and children. After they were divorced, XYZ sued the generous brother to recover what the marriage venture had cost him. The Massachusetts court decided in his favor, costing the brother a pretty penny.

Not a few people oppose the presently growing no-fault concept when terminating the marriage contract. They believe that we are marching backward toward the customs of primitive or pagan societies wherein divorce was considered to be a private affair, with scarcely a legal marker to guide the participants, demanding few formalities and no, or almost no, governmental supervision.

Quasi and
Same-Sex
Marriage

Legal rights and duties between husband and wife have been well stylized during the past centuries. But legal relationships between men and women living together without benefit of clergy and legal relationships between homosexuals are in a state of flux. As a result, wise contracts between people living unconventionally are more necessary than for the conventional majority for whom legal and property affairs have been well charted.

As distilled from the dictionaries and as understood by the multitude, marriage is a procedure under which a *man* and a *woman* may establish their decision to live together as husband and wife by making legal and often religious commitments to that effect. Every lexicon which I have examined shows a duality of sexes in this connection. Consequently, while an unmarried heterosexual couple can quickly metamorphose into a "true" marriage whenever the partners so desire, a pair of homosexuals who set up housekeeping cannot do so. Presently in all of the United States, there is a legal as well as a biological difference in kind between heterosexual and homosexual relationships.

It would be convenient if the vocabulary included specialized words to differentiate the two quite different situations. I submit that for heterosexuals the term should be "quasi-marriage" and for homosexuals, "same-sex marriage."

The Latin word *quasi* means "as if," "as though," "in a certain sense or degree." In the language of the law, the term "quasi" is familiarly linked with contract; a quasi-contract comes into being when persons who have not expressly contracted with each other nevertheless become obligated because of their acts and fragmentary assertions accompanied by reliance, one or both upon the other. *Webster's New International Dictionary* links "quasi" with about 1000 words—quasi-absolute to quasi-zeal. But I do not find "quasi-marriage" or "quasi-spouse."

"Quasi-marriage" seems to be the best available term to apply generally to the growing plethora of relationships outside marriage between men and women. Often men and women live together with no attempt to conceal the fact that there has been no marriage contract or ceremony. There is no neighborhood assertion that "we are husband and wife" as in the case of the common-law marriages described in the section "The Betrothal." Indeed, there may be a braggadocio attitude: "We are not married; we do not believe in it; we are free!"

Shortly, brief mention will be made of the desire of an apparently expanding number of homosexuals to marry—thus converting the historical meaning of marriage (i.e., between members of the opposite sex) to include marriage contracts between persons of the same sex. The term "same-sex marriages" has been used in a writing by a United States district judge who would permit them.

Caveat—warning

The term *caveat* means "warning." I state this caveat in the strongest terms. It applies to informal heterosexual affairs and with even greater force to homosexual liaisons. When reviewing contracts predicated upon or stemming from any of these activities, some of which are presently unlawful and punishable as crimes, we are treating a mostly unmarked road planted with legal mines.

Unconventional conduct ranges from adultery (forbidden in the Ten Commandments and today by the laws of many countries and of almost all our fifty states) to fornication—intercourse between unmarrieds—which is *not* a crime in some states but is in others. The end result is that, when living in a jurisdiction which has *not* made fornication a crime, a heterosexual couple may live together and, much as they may offend the mores of the vicinity, they are not considered criminal merely because of their cohabitation. In other states they may be.

How strictly the law is enforced raises another set of questions. Though the laws of a state may be severe, the gendarmes of a metropolitan district may have no time and little inclination to search out love nests. They leave that vexing problem to landladies and the neighbors. In a village in the same state, the constable may have a heritage of several puritanical generations. If the prosecuting attorney is of like mind, conduct acceptable within the sophisticated city may be considered criminal in the hinterland.

This must be said with firmness: Couples who choose to flaunt the law or even the mores of the community in which they dwell should not enter into any written contracts which are predicated on their personal relationships. Even if their proposed contract is for some lawful purpose—such as ownership of property or allocation of income or the division of household expenses between "roommates"—the recitals of the document should not reveal their illicit relationship. Their business and property affairs should be insulated from the conduct upon which society frowns.

To restate: Homosexuals are entitled to make lawful contracts. But they should seek the best legal advice available and ask counsel to make sure that their otherwise lawful commitments are not fatally affected because their possibly illicit relationship is revealed above their signatures. A naïvely drawn covenant may convict someone of a crime. What should not be said may be as important as what may properly be written.

There are fifty states; what can lawfully be accomplished in one jurisdiction may be wrongful in another—just as formerly in thirty states interracial marriages were forbidden.

There is an ancillary aspect of contracts between unconventionals and between one, or more of them, and other persons —with "third parties" as a lawyer is apt to say. This is the temptation to be less than candid, to hide, to dissimulate, to prevaricate—adding up to a record of recitals which will support a charge of fraud. To give but three examples:

1. A participant in an extramarital heterosexual arrange-

ment may apply for a desirable job. The application blank inquires as to marital status. Applicant occupies an apartment with a "friend" of the opposite sex. Though somewhat suspicious, the house manager and cotenants accept them as married. The tenants and manager rationalize that to preserve her professional identity, the woman uses her maiden name on the directory.

How shall the applicant check the line: "Married? . . . Single? . . . Divorced? . . ." And what about the interview with the personnel director who thinks stability a prime requisite for the position which is open. The truthful answer is of course "single," perhaps flanked by "divorced." They are not inconsistent.

But how is the "single" answer to be explained when the routine check by the personnel department reveals two names —opposite sexes—for the same apartment? If, anticipating an investigation as a condition precedent to acceptance for so important a post, the applicant checked "married," he or she has lied. Without elaboration, a letter or telephone call from a subordinate in the personnel office says, "We have no place for you," softened only by "regrets."

2. They wish to buy a house. As will be seen shortly, *between themselves*, they have optional ways of holding title and making a record of their division of ownership rights. Now we are discussing purchasing procedures. An ad invites prospective buyers to call the owners—"save the real estate commission." It is an attractive house in a pleasant upper-middle-class district. Most of the neighbors have lived there for years. The owners would not think of bringing in a discordant element to discomfort their lifelong friends.

If applicants go together, from the viewpoint of the owners, they must be (1) husband and wife or (2) about to be married. If they tell the truth, the owners will await the next prospects. If one goes alone, what is his or her reason for buying a seven-room house for single occupancy? Again there is a pressure to dissimulate, the end results of which will not be good.

The familiar refrain of Sir Walter Scott—"Oh, what a tangled web we weave / When first we practice to deceive"— is of course trite. But unfortunately it is true, especially when applied to persons entering into contractual relationships.

If somehow the pair buys a house by deception, the antipathy of prying self-righteous neighbors may prove unpleasant.

3. An economic (job) example and a domestic (place to dwell) example have been given of typical problems faced by participants in quasi and same-sex marriages when dealing with the square world. Engaging in public affairs, voluntary or political, involves handicaps, some openly and frankly stated. Some whispered. To run for a public office is natural to a young lawyer who dreams of a sequence: deputy prosecuting attorney (to gain name familiarity by winning a few murder or rape cases); then prosecuting attorney; then to the state legislature; and then to the United States Congress or a judgeship. What shall the lawyer tell the voters during the first campaign? The truth foreordains defeat. A lie will later leak out and wreck his or her career.

The broad caveat concerning possible punishment under criminal statutes was based only on the illicit relationship. Because every business and contractual relationship may be affected, it seems right to mention a few concomitant hazards to both parties. One may find person and property charged with liability because of the conduct, civil or criminal, of the other—without the safeguards the law builds around the marital relationship. If one partner goes sour, the other may be dragged into the imbroglio under accusations of principal and agent, conspiracy, even an accessory—helping out after the deed was done—and other theories under which one may be implicated in another's criminal conduct or held liable for civil obligations. Dope was discovered in the apartment; to whom did it belong? Did both have knowledge of it?

Heterosexual arrangements

In some quasi-marriages, more than two are involved in an overlapping, intertwined, heterosexual relationship. Babies are born and, as decreed by nature, become children and then adults. They are reared, perhaps by the natural parents, or by one of them, or perhaps principally by someone else. The child may not know who is the true father; nor may the mother be sure.

What are the child's rights in respect to support, schooling, and eventually, inheritance?

If they acknowledge any social and parental duties, unmarried couples living together and begetting children should have contracts setting forth their mutual responsibilities and property rights.

The comment is similar if no children come. In due time the dual or multiple relationship will be terminated, by death if not before. Who owns the property which has been accumulated? The astute man or woman who is a money-maker and saver may have substantial assets in his or her name, despite socially unacceptable views on marriage and sex. Do quasi-spouses have legally enforceable property rights? Title to the suburban five-acre tract on which the clan lives and grows crops for home consumption and casual sale was taken in the name of the dominant male, as an anthropologist might put it. There being a religious overtone, he is revered by his "family" as would be a prophet. There are no serious objections from the half dozen or more who work and contribute funds to the project; the women forget their rights.

Can he convey marketable title if they choose to sell at a huge profit and move farther from the city? If the funds are not immediately funneled into a new homestead, to whom does the money belong; how should it be divided? The chieftain is mortal. To whom descend the properties of the commune: land, cars, bank accounts, and other assets held in his name?

These questions, and others, have been before the courts in various frameworks. It is a fair forecast that unless, invisibly, the "freedom" cycle has reached its peak and we are about to return to more puritanical marital customs, there will be a host of court decisions and spasmodic legislation, probably confusing, as is the legislative paradigm.

Absent a clear contract or legislation, what, for example, should the answers be to these questions:

Who enjoys the beneficial ownership of the property, or the proceeds thereof? (By "beneficial ownership" is meant for whose benefit the property—any kind of property—is really intended, regardless of who is named as owner.)

How shall the properties be divided among the beneficial owners?

What is the participation of those who did not go forth and earn, but tilled the land, attended to household duties, and watched the children irrespective of parenthood?

And the inevitable, to whom does the property pass in the event of the death of the person who holds title?

The questions are fundamentally the same if there are but two living as quasi-spouses, whether or not children come.

A natural answer is: "The judge should divide the property and mandate liability for the maintenance of children as is equitable under the circumstances." Or the wording may be: "Awards should be made and duties imposed according to the conscience of the chancellor—the judge." But these statements are akin to lofty objectives, rather than rules to guide the court as decisions are made. The conscience of the judge who sits in room 710 may differ sharply from that of the judge who presides a short walk down the hall and around the corner in room 770.

There must be rules—theories—to which to tie if there is to be any consistency as innumerable cases come and go. A carefully drawn contract will give the answers, and there should be no need of controversy in court.

It is apparent that we are discussing couples, or "families," small or large—companions who expect some permanence. Eliminated are weekenders and those who gather for a saturnalia, or a series of them. The attorney representing the quasi-marital more or less permanent clan can develop suitable contract arrangements regarding property under one or more of several legal approaches:

1. *A Trust Relationship.* A "trust" is created when one or more persons (including corporate persons, such as a bank) hold title to property, real or personal, for the benefit of the persons or institutions on whose behalf the trust was formed. "Real" refers to land, buildings, and other things appurtenant to the land. Sometimes it is hard to be sure which is which if the instrument (often called "Deed of Trust") is not meticulously drawn. Personalty comprehends everything except real estate. Stocks, bonds, bank accounts, furniture, TV, and other assets (a hot-water heater or furnace attached to the home?). In Roman law the word was "movables"—more descriptive, I think, than our "personalty."

It is not difficult for an attorney familiar with trusts and estate planning to compose a suitable trust agreement, whether for two people living together in an apartment or two dozen living somewhat as an ancient clan, in a commune.

He or she who holds legal title to common possessions of two people does so as trustee for the other, the beneficiary, according to their agreed shares. Or the trustee or trustees may hold title for the benefit of many, and their successors. If the venture is designed to be permanent, there might be two or three trustees with provisions for succession. The proportionate interests of the beneficial owners would be spelled out, with formulas to take care of those who leave. Duties would be assumed by those who become beneficiaries. Some participants might have substantial resources to contribute to the venture, others not. So proportions would differ, or those with substantial assets might be glad to donate them to the common cause. Any conceivable variations can be spelled out, leaving no reason for later disputes and bitterness.

2. *A Partnership Relationship.*   The legal possibilities of a partnership agreement are great, so long as we are concerned with property rights, participation in profits and losses, management, and so on. Sex relationships are beyond judicial jurisdiction.

3. *A Cooperative Enterprise.*   Again, and always emphasizing that a stencil cannot be developed to control their personal relationships, under the laws of many states cooperative associations may be organized for farming and other productive purposes. Weaving, pottery (with a roadside stand as an adjunct to the enterprise), unique furniture—as a practical matter, almost anything not directly competitive with the mass-production industries—is adaptable to and may be very efficient in cooperative form.

Each member of the cooperative would own a fair share, and shifts in membership could be handled expeditiously.

4. *Joint-ownership Agreements.*   The area of the law pertaining to the joint ownership of property is a maze. The legal words commonly used are "tenancy" or "tenant," not "ownership" or "owners." To compound confusion, laws differ from state to state. Legal terminology includes: joint tenancy; tenants in common; tenancy at sufferance or, in sharp contrast, *joint tenancy with the right of survivorship*; and tenants in severalty. That, surely, is enough to mystify. But for a cherry on the sundae, out of the many available, I cannot resist adding the poetic "tenant in tail ex provisione virl" and "tenant paravaile."

The nub of this recital is indicated by the clause in italics: joint tenancies with the right of survivorship. If the companions are few in number, a joint-ownership agreement, with right of survivorship, backed by wills, may be a suitable solution. The name pretty well defines the meaning. Mae and Joseph or more own the property together. Upon the death of one of them, the property passes to the survivor or survivors.

Joint tenancies with the right of survivorship sound simple and attractive. But many a law article has been written pointing out pitfalls. For the two or more who are merging property interests, the cue is to listen to competent advice, with all the facts on the table, and decide what course is best in their factual framework. I suspect that the possibilities of a legally established cooperative (item 3, above) are too often overlooked.

5. *Support of Children.* Some of the adult companions may be habitual drifters. Should they be on the dotted line in respect to the support of children? The practical point may be raised that such a contract would be worthless paper; the obligor has no steady job and no reachable assets. Perhaps he himself cannot be found.

But that would not always be so. A man unwilling to be tied by the bonds of matrimony might be willing to commit himself to support a child, whether his own or not, if for a time he has been living *in loco parentis*. He need not acknowledge parenthood if he has doubts about it.

6. *Contracts Regarding Wills.* The person in whose name clan property is lodged may die. To whom does the property go? If decedent left a valid will, the property subject to the testamentary document will be distributed as therein directed. The word "valid" is broadly used. It refers not only to form and the formalities (witness: declaration of testamentary intent) but also substance. A person living in a commune may have a spouse elsewhere; they had not completed their divorce proceeding. Or decedent may leave a legitimate child; or one illegitimate, but parenthood has been acknowledged. Failure to provide for them may invalidate the will, in whole or in part.

The members of the informal family will do well to make sure that the trusted leader who holds title to their assets is contractually bound to execute and keep in effect a will which distributes the property of the companions in accordance with their plan. This comment applies to all the routes discussed: trusts, partnerships, cooperatives, joint ownerships, and any arrangement, by whatever name it is called.

Homosexual marriages

Homosexuality, occasionally called "sexual inversion," may be tersely defined as the sexual attraction of a person to one of the same sex. The term "homosexual" comprehends both male and female. "Lesbianism," connoting female homosexuality, traces to the island of Lesbos, home of the Greek poetess Sappho. During the first half of the sixth century B.C. she was the leader of an association of women bound together by tenacious homosexual affection. Since in current parlance lesbianism is included in the broader term "homosexual," with but one exception there will be no need of using it again.

In this illumination of same-sex marriages, mention must be made of contracts between homosexuals who consider themselves married—despite the hearty disapproval of the conservatives of the community and sanctions imposed by law.

Occasionally homosexual couples have asserted their right to be married, as are heterosexual lovers. They have applied to the appropriate public officers for a marriage license. Single-sex lawful *marriage* is the status for which they strive, contending that as citizens they possess the constitutional right. When used in relation to homosexuals, the words "married" and "marriage" may sometimes be put between quotation marks to differentiate them from the legally recognized heterosexual relationship.

1. *Legality of Homosexual Marriage Contracts.*   From time to time, many if not most human societies have registered disapproval of homosexuality, some vigorously. However, reputable scholars specializing in the study of earlier civilizations report that out of the seventy-six studied, forty-nine (64 percent) accepted the practice as normal.

In the modern world, the American tradition of intense antagonism to homosexuality between consenting adults stands somewhat alone. The majority viewpoint in Scandinavia, in Switzerland, the Netherlands, and here and there elsewhere, is said to be one of tolerance. Perhaps in part because of these different viewpoints, today in our land, the question of whether homosexuals should be allowed to marry is being asked by sociologists and members of related disciplines and has been before courts for judicial determination. Inconceivable a few years ago, a plausible legal argument can now be made to the effect that single-sex marriages are constitutionally lawful and cannot be forbidden by a legislative body. Some scholars believe that the United States Supreme Court has already taken a step in that direction, or at least opened the door to an unbiased consideration of the problem.

The decision is appropriately named *Loving* v. *the State of Virginia*. Formerly, in about three-fifths of the then forty-eight states, statutes forbade interracial marriages. As late as 1967, when the *Loving* controversy was decided, the prohibition was still in the books of fourteen states.

Virginia law was clear to the effect that when a black and white left the state to be married in a jurisdiction permitting interracial marriages and then returned to Virginia as husband and wife, they would be guilty of a crime. Mildred Jeter and Richard Perry Loving did just that. They were convicted in the courts of Virginia. The United States Supreme Court set aside the convictions, holding that marriage is one of the basic civil rights of man. The freedom to marry, or not to marry, a person of another race resides within the individual and cannot be prohibited by the state.

If a legislature cannot bar marriages on the basis of race, ask the homosexuals, how can it do so under a sexual classification?

There are other decisions of the United States Supreme Court in which homosexuals find solace. One is *Estelle T. Griswold and others* v. *the State of Connecticut*. A Connecticut statute made the use of contraceptives a criminal offense. Personnel of the Planned Parenthood League were convicted of violations. Reversing the Connecticut courts, the Supreme

Court found zones of privacy into which government may not intrude. At the very least, say the advocates of same-sex marriages, this decision is a straw in the wind now blowing in their favor toward an ultimate decision that sex cannot be a factor in determining legal rights—anymore than can race.

Another very small straw in the wind is a recent decision of the Supreme Court of Nebraska. The case went as follows: The city of Grand Island prohibited more than one person in a "household" from being on the city payroll at the same time. For several years the groom had been employed as a mechanic in the department of public works. For a similar period the bride had a position in the police department. Their duties did not overlap.

Calling attention to the law, the city manager asked that one or the other resign from employment by Grand Island. Both refused. He fired the groom. They brought suit. The Nebraska court ruled that the city had established a system of classification which impinged upon the fundamental right to marry. There was no claim of discrimination on the basis of sex; bride and groom were treated alike. The constitutionally unpermissible rule was an inhibition of the fundamental right to marry. If there is such a fundamental right, "Why," ask homosexuals, "can't we marry?"

Splinter groups within the Episcopal Church—the most formal of all Protestant denominations—have adopted the deviant philosophy. An avowed homosexual woman was ordained a deacon. The diaconate is the initial of the three ordained orders. Deacons in that church are authorized to baptize, preach, and perform marriage ceremonies. If that trend within conservative Episcopalian cloisters continues, a court may one day confront two homosexuals who assert they have been formally married by a homosexual deacon before the altar at the cathedral. And what God has joined together, let no judge put asunder.

Appellate courts of at least four states (Kentucky, Minnesota, New York, and Washington) have squarely faced the question of whether there can be a valid marriage between persons of the same sex. The cases arise in different factual frameworks; hence the approach and reasoning of the judges differ. But the essence of all is that the relationship called "marriage" has always been the union of a man and woman as husband and wife. The fact that the legislature has not expressly forbidden homosexual marriages does not make permissible a marital contract between persons biologically of the same sex. Their constitutional rights were not impaired when the county clerk refused to issue a marriage license.

If the *Loving* case is a weather vane, in respect to same-sex marriages, it has been bypassed in the state of Washington in that regard. Counsel representing the homosexuals urged the court that it is a precedent supporting them.

Deciding against them, the Washington judges reasoned that an impermissible sexual discrimination does not underlie a prohibition of same-sex marriages. Refusing to recognize them goes to the very nature and definition of marriage itself.

That holding is criticized by a distinguished federal district judge and his law clerk writing for a lawyers' magazine. They believe that the *Loving* case does support the arguments of the homosexuals that unisex marriages should be permitted without express statutory sanction.

Ancillary arguments which homosexuals believe support their claim for constitutional equality include discrimination in measuring taxes—income (both state and federal), estate, and inheritance. Despite the sociologists, I believe that when the test comes, the Supreme Court of the United States will say that the type of marriage which is the right of everyone is marriage in its usual sense—between male and female. There is no constitutional inhibition *against* marriage between homosexuals. But to sanctify such a novel concept is a legislative, not a judicial, function. It must be left to the legislatures and courts of each state to decide whether the traditional meaning of the word "marriage" shall be changed to include unisex marriages. The day may come when the legislatures and courts of certain states flash a green light, while in the other jurisdictions it stays red.

2. *Other Contracts between Homosexuals.* When homosexuals deem themselves married, whether permanently or at will, certain contracts between themselves as individuals become worthy of consideration.

There are sharp distinctions between the contractual program of homosexual marriages and heterosexual marriages, whether true or quasi. One of them is that homosexual marriages do not produce children. Except when unalterably forbidden by advanced years, disease, or deformity, any heterosexual marriage may result in offspring. Were it not for other complicating factors, contracts between homosexuals could be quite simple—no children or grandchildren to worry about, except: (1) in an extremely rare ménage resulting from a lawful adoption; (2) when a lesbian partner brings forth a child conceived outside the continuing homosexual relationship; (3) when a homosexual has custody of a child by a previously orthodox heterosexual marriage. The last is not a rare occurrence.

Assume two lesbians who want to be married or believe that their relationship is the equivalent of marriage. What sort of contracts should they consider? Here we are thinking only of property. It is a stable union, and they accumulate assets. The law ignores them as married in respect to intestacies (i.e., what happens to property when one dies without a will). If one dies intestate, property in her name may pass to her blood relatives, leaving her lover entirely out unless a survivor can prove a trust, a partnership, or other lawful contractual relationship, such as a binding agreement to make a will, already discussed.

There is no need here to repeat the inventories of property possibilities listed in the sections "Prenuptial Agreements," "Agreements during Marriage," and "Estate Planning; Trusts" as well as earlier in this section. They constitute a checklist for all varieties of personal relationships. If one out of five, indeed if only one idea applies, a careful review of the lists may pay off handsomely for unmarrieds considering a contractual relationship. A separation agreement might become of consequence. Who gets what if they break up?

Mention should be made of the plight of the unmarried companion of superstars—tremendous earners—and likewise of anyone who has for a period of time kept house while the other produced living expenses for both, and saved even a small pot of gold. In the absence of any agreement, should the court find an *implied* arrangement which will justify a division between them? Legal theories to which the judge can tie have been discussed.

The typical moneymaker (TV, athletic, or movie star, or business tycoon) is the vivid example. It is vital to his or her public image that sexual eccentricities be kept secret. The stars are as discreet as a CIA operative is supposed to be. Some who are bisexual maintain the façade of a home and perhaps a child or two to demonstrate that he or she is a "straight."

The courts will protect the home and children to the greatest extent the law permits. But most judges will show little sympathy for the secret companion. The question is being asked whether, at least when dealing with astronomical income and potential accumulations, should there not be a rule of law giving some financial protection to the disfavored appendage of a rich celebrity? Perhaps the satellite of the celebrity should be permitted compensation for current "services" with generous provisions for termination pay when the affections of the celebrity change.

Due warning has already been given. Agreements arising from or predicated upon illicit affairs must be worded with exquisite care. The lawful, even laudable purpose of the contract may be unfavorably affected by the beyond-the-law relationships. Counsel will suggest appropriate language to accomplish the desired lawful purpose in respect to property and property rights by avoiding references to the relationship and will not predicate the agreement upon it.

His Hers

5

Agreements
during
Marriage

It would be whimsical indeed to intimate that out of the hundreds of business concurrences between a husband and wife, many should be formalized by a written contract. In a scholastic sense they enter into a "contract" whenever they determine a source of funds for this enterprise or that or an allocation of earnings. When the project is a big one (a new home or second automobile), many spouses do recognize that they have made a business agreement. The new car or house may be definitely earmarked as "hers"; contracts of purchase, deeds, bills of sale, and certificates of ownership are issued accordingly.

Indulging in the presumption that an earner husband who supports a socially or civically active wife retains at least a mild veto power financially, please view the contractual problems of a new fur coat. He finally gives in, saying: "It is too expensive; it does not sound like a sale price to me. The furs which Aunt Ida gave you are still as good as any in the neighborhood. But if that particular coat means so much to you, buy it. That will be your combined birthday and Christmas present." Here we have a specific contractual authority, an agency to buy the coat, albeit oral. It is a simple affair, done with when the bill is paid next month. A thank-you plus a kiss from her closes the covenant. Had she been a wealthy wife with habitual no-limit charge accounts, she might have had an implied power to buy the four-figure luxury fur garment on credit, without authorization from him. Nearly every wife may lawfully charge ordinary family requirements without express authority from the husband.

Ownerships

There are occasions during a marriage where a formal, written contract might prove to be a blessing and prevent later misunderstandings. Such occasions arise incident to property and business affairs, even though neither spouse is conscious of marital dissension, present or potential. Illustrations abound:

Suppose John has a steady job with DuPont, at a salary sufficient for the needs of Jane and their children, and hopes that one day he will be superintendent of a modest segment of the corporate empire with a fine retirement plan in prospect. But while content, he is not enraptured by his position in the big city. Almost secretly, he dreams of returning to a farming community like that of his youth. He would have horses and could hunt and fish. Jane's father, a widower, dies suddenly, age fifty-six. His estate is such that his family farm (not yet fully developed and short of the best equipment) could go to Jane alone, if she surrendered her share of the securities and father's other savings to her sisters and brother.

John had worked on farms during summer vacations and for one full year between high school and college. He thought he would make good as manager and worker No. 1 on Jane's farm. So did Jane. They took the plunge. John made good; in due time there was a prosperous enterprise, periodic crop failures notwithstanding.

Thirty years later, to whom should this farm really belong? The man behind the desk at a title insurance or abstract company would say that the records at the county courthouse clearly show the land and buildings are Jane's separate property. John has no interest therein, except as to the 80 additional acres they bought a few years ago. Most of their savings have gone into the farm—buildings, twin silos, and expensive specialized equipment.

For the first time during their forty-five years of marriage, Jane and John have fundamental divergences of opinion in respect to property matters. Jane has convictions as to the disposition of the farm in her will. John differs and says that no, after thirty years of toil, the land, not merely the equipment, is as much his as hers. He wants a will quite different from the one Jane has in mind.

Is it not manifest that prior to withdrawing from the safety of John's post with DuPont, there should have been a carefully drawn agreement covering John's efforts vis-à-vis Jane's inheritance, as affecting the ownership of the land, the buildings, and possibly specialized equipment?

For this next illustration, both husband and wife are working; Myrtle has a better position and earns more than Fred. Suddenly Fred inherits his family's long-established neighborhood hardware store. Fred had worked there most Saturdays and vacations until he finished school. Then he emigrated to the big city 2000 miles away where he and Myrtle now live. Should Myrtle give up her good position and become a working partner in Fred's store without a firm agreement as to the ownership of the business? Neither doubts their ability to carry on profitably. Fred, they think, will blossom. Instead of working at a routine job, he will be a businessman with a two-generation prestige in a pleasant suburban community. The family will be on a higher plateau. So they move and never regret the decision.

But who *owns* the store? Fred in his separate estate by virtue of his inheritance? If Myrtle is to work in the store (perhaps also doing some of the bookkeeping in the evenings, after the housework is done) should she not also be one of the owners, as would a partner?

Or suppose another family decides it desirable to buy a capital asset which looms large in relation to family resources. A new or second home, a business or an interest therein, an outside enterprise believed to have great potential or to be of exceptional value to the husband in his affairs, or even a luxury, such as a sizable ketch. As to the house and ketch, the route is easy. If the wife's money pays the purchase price, take title in her name *in her separate estate*.

But it may not be compatible with the husband's business relationships for the wife to have an avowed separate ownership interest in certain of the ventures of the husband. Then lend him the money; take a formal promissory note as evidence of the debt and secure it as best the law allows. The husband, if truly wise, will wish her to have separate counsel of her choice to scrutinize the documents from the viewpoint of the wife.

Even a simple unsecured note may have great value. It may prevent failures in memory. It makes clear who owns the $20,000. For example, it might cut that much from the husband's estate and save thousands of dollars in taxes, depending upon his top inheritance and estate tax bracket.

Or perhaps the wife is the primary entrepreneur. Then the illustrations should be reversed.

So far, the suggestion of this section has been: Whenever there are substantial separate assets which significantly affect the family's way of life, whether acquired before or acquired after marriage, the possible desirability of contractual avoidance of potential controversy as to ownership of property (real cr personal) should be explored.

It is rare that, between spouses, a contract of "joint tenancy with the right of survivorship" regarding land assumes the importance it may often have between the quasi- and same-sex marrieds (see "Quasi and Same-Sex Marriage"). Divorce does not "in and of itself," rules the Supreme Court of Maine, affect a joint tenancy between husband and wife. The land retains its status as joint-tenancy property.

Occasionally, situations occur where it may be advantageous to segregate or contractually change the title to property within the family. On the other hand, a happily married matron who has from time to time received substantial inheritances read the first draft of this chapter. She has always put her wealth into the family "pot" (as she calls it) and believes her policy of undiluted fiscal unity has paid high dividends in harmony between her and her husband. They discuss investments and other money policies together on the basis that everything is *ours*, not some of it mine alone merely because it was bequeathed to me. Consistent with this viewpoint, during the early years of their marriage, she felt that she had an equal right to participate and to make decisions in respect to the disposition of her husband's military salary, which was then their only income.

However, usually in connection with programming to minimize death dues (federal and state), contracts concerning the ownership of properties may be advantageous yet may not have been covered in the prenuptial agreement, if any. Contracts between spouses changing the ownership of their properties should be entered into warily, with the advice of counsel skilled in this field and with the blessing of the certified public accountant, if the family uses one. "Warily" does not connote mistrust as between husband and wife, though they should be sure this is best also for each. The caveat "warily" was used in respect to the outside world: the tax gatherers; creditors of one or both of the spouses; parties with whom they, or either of them, have ongoing contractual relationships; parties to future contracts, still over the horizon; in short, anyone who may assert claims against members of the family.

Despite their relative rarity, it would be impossible to catalog and analyze all, or even a fair representation, of typical situations where an effective agreement between spouses changing the ownership of their property is advisable. The sagacious suggestion is this: If and when a recommendation comes to change property ownership within the family, whether at a bridge table or from a banker, consult competent professionals. Make sure of the possible effect on children and perhaps grandchildren, as well as upon husband and wife.

Similarly, it would be a disservice to purport to draft patterns for contracts concerning intra (within)–family ownerships. There are too many variables. A fundamental is: What state? Is it one of the forty-two common-law states or one of the eight community-property states wherein live over 40 million people, or is some of the property within one jurisdiction (state) and some in another?

In addition to the fundamental of "what law governs" are questions of relative age, health, and the educational requirements of children. Consider what is being *given up* by one of the spouses—including a strong personal desire to live in one locality as contrasted with another, and so on indefinitely. The prophesied dollar gain of the proposed project does not encompass all involved. This is a situation requiring a carefully developed checklist before asking a lawyer to draw a contract. It saves his time. He will bring up legal and tax advantages and disadvantages. Your checklist should cover every facet which affects the family personally as well as financially. These include anticipated income and capital buildup as well as the proposed change contrasted with continuing the family's present way of life—for example, one of the spouses giving up a permanent position with opportunity for advancement in order to give the other what is believed to be a better chance elsewhere.

Loans

Sometimes both husband and wife own significant property at the time of their marriage or acquire it later by inheritance or gift. Assume the husband has a going business, possibly hazardous. He needs more capital. If the wife is willing to commit her funds to the husband's business, perhaps it should be by way of a loan, clearly set up as such, and secured by the best security device the law makes available to the transaction. The bank and others who finance the business should have actual knowledge of it. The borrowing husband should *want* her to enjoy the peace of mind of a secured creditor as to her participation. She will have worries enough about his risks.

A loan secured by an enforceable security device, as suggested in the preceding paragraph, will handicap the husband when arranging a line of credit at the bank or with an essential supplier. There, a subordinated loan from the wife might be a workable compromise. The documents say that her loan is secondary to the First National Bank and to the XYZ Manufacturing Company. Thus she retains her position as a creditor, though not of the first rank. She should make it clear she will not dip further into her separate funds to pay her busband's business debts—unless, of course, she later is willing to do so. And there lies the risk. An irresistible temptation to try to salvage a lost cause with good money.

Interest should not be nominal; a creditor might claim there has been an investment—a contribution to capital—rather than a loan. Neither does the rent the business pays for the use of the wife's funds need to be the highest commercial rate, particularly during periods of tight money.

A negation of contract may be worthy of thought. Again assume a wife with substantial property, inherited from members of her family or a former husband, or made on her own. She has discovered that her husband (otherwise quite satisfactory) has a tendency to jump from this project to that, always falling short of his expectations. Now and then she is required to sign a document; she is told there is no intention to obligate her separate property. This worries her. She has heard of wives who unexpectedly, against their protests, have seen their own funds go down the drain.

Her attorney might approve a rubber stamp which she uses below her name whenever pressed to sign a paper along with her husband. If in a common-law state, it could read: "Wife signs to show acquiescence in respect to her interest in her husband's property. She in no way obligates her separate property." In a community-property state, it might read: "Wife signs to bind community property only—*not* her separate estate."

Or she might persuade her husband to agree *never* to enter into a venture except when shielded by a corporation, in which she owns no stock. If the husband says her signature is required when guaranteeing a corporate obligation, she should use her rubber stamp.

Partnerships and joint ventures

Husband and wife can informally be in business together (the delicatessen shop) or they may be formal partners in an enterprise of great magnitude. Here, as in other commercial affairs between spouses, proper contracts serve a dual purpose: (1) they set forth the business relationships so that operating disputes will be minimized (was that last $10,000 advanced by the wife a loan or a contribution to capital?) and (2) because the terms are—or should be—clear and available for reference, they help insulate commerce from domestic dispute. The husband and wife have a better chance of enjoying the best of two worlds.

Partnership contracts are not the easiest to write. There are often many more aspects to cover than, for contrast, usually found in a contract for the sale of a carload of apples or a thousand dozen manufactured gadgets. A partnership may involve personal as well as dollar problems, particularly when between husband and wife; or when the wife is one of several partners. Who is to be the managing partner and what will be the peripheries of managerial authority?

Where serious friction develops in a husband-wife business or professional partnership, the expectable options are: (1) continue the marriage, one withdrawing entirely from the enterprise, or (2) sell out and continue the marriage, or (3) dissolve the marriage and continue together the partnership activities, or (4) close the eyes to reality and carry on both at home and abroad.

Route (1) is feasible, particularly if the retiring partner develops an individual venture. So, of course, is route (2). Route (4) invites chaos and eventually divorce. So does route (3) unless one or both are soon happily remarried. Recently divorced spouses would find it hard to work together as impersonal partners, except in most unusual circumstances. I suppose successful public entertainers are all unusual when contrasted with mundane business and square professional careers. The headlines of a recent newspaper feature story derived from *The New York Times* reads, "Couples Didn't Divorce Jobs." Then, referring to it as the "Ultimate Civilized Relationship," the writer, Judy Klemesrud, lists and quotes husband-wife entertainment teams who go on performing together after divorce. She predicts that there will be more. So it can be done.

However, here is a classic example of the expectable; it is not fiction. The spouses owned a struggling factory; he ran it. The ledger showed little hope, though the owners both believed it could be made to pay. The wife took a condensed course in bookkeeping and went to work in the office, thereby saving a salary.

Came Pearl Harbor. The husband was a lieutenant jg in the Naval Reserve. He put on his uniform and sailed to the South Pacific. She took over the business. Almost at once it prospered, by leaps and bounds, though it was not a war-related industry. There was no reason to believe it would be hurt by the treaty which was signed on the foredeck of the *Missouri*. He came home a full commander with a fine array of ribbons, ready to take over. I put it squarely to them.

This is not the *kind* of business the Commander can run; he would do well at something else, as proved by his war record. Neither can the factory succeed with two at the helm. They must make a choice: (1) she continue to run the enterprise and he find another occupation, (2) she withdraw from the business and he take over for the few years it would survive under his management, or (3) they run the business together until both home and business crack up. She replied that the bank, suppliers, and customers had all come to rely on her; as a matter of honor she could not leave. He insisted that he is the head of the family and would take over, she having charge of all accounting. She gave in. A few years later the program ended with bankruptcy and divorce. They simply could not work and live together. This is a story to be remembered as spouses become business associates or partners. Twenty-four hours a day may be twelve too many.

For the purpose of this discussion, a joint venture or, as often called, a joint adventure, may be defined as a partnership for a limited purpose or period. It is a trap for the gullible husband or wife, particularly the latter because often the husband is the business activist. He is the one who comes home with this wonderful scheme whereby all participants will wax rich. I am not speaking of a steady, permanent business. The reference is an adventure: in land, often including subdivision and the speculative building of houses; in a hazardous construction project, such as a bridge; in the formation of a syndicate to buy high-flyer stocks; in advancing funds to develop a patent. In short, I refer to an enterprise which usually meets the meaning of the very name by which it happens to be called, "venture" or "adventure." It is an undertaking attended with risk; it takes disproportionate chances.

I called it a "trap" because it sounds less formidable than a permanent partnership. The wife may commit funds to this fun-sounding, joint, short-term venture without the formalities (protection) she would insist upon if she were investing in or lending her separate funds to a permanent business partnership with her husband alone, or with him and others.

A husband and wife chaffering with each other in respect to committing funds to a joint adventure limited to one project should realize that its dollar demands may grow and soon they may be throwing away good money in the hope of salvaging a sinking ship. The resources of the family exchequer may be exhausted. If she wants to insulate her separate funds from the ultimate risks of the venture, she should insist on a firmly secured loan or, at very least, a limited partnership under the provisions of which she would not be liable to creditors and need lose no more than she originally invested.

Employment

There is a trade term "mom-and-pop shop." Before the supermarket scoured the field, there were many mom-and-pop groceries, perhaps with living quarters above or in back. There are still a few. Dry-cleaning establishments, little restaurants, gift or antique shops, and other retail units persist. There are many "in-house" factories, manned solely, or nearly so, by members of the family. They usually produce components sold to concerns which incorporate them in larger devices.

Until comparatively recently it would seldom have occurred to either mom or pop that one is working for the other; often they are not; it is an unwritten partnership arrangement. Within-the-family economic activity is not limited to mom-and-pop units. There are larger and more exalted activities.

Suppose the bride owns and operates a travel or advertising agency, a profitable boutique, a beauty shop, a bookstore, or whatever enterprise she developed on her own or took over upon the death of her parents. Granted that there might be fewer problems if she employed an outsider, she could use the groom in the business. Perhaps she first met him when, guided by Kismet, he applied there for work prior to the parents' passing.

An explicit employment contract may be useful in many of the myriad situations where one spouse owns a business, whether individually or through ownership of stock in a close corporation (only one or very few stockholders) and the other spouse works there. That means in writing; otherwise the commercial relationship, perhaps including the very ownership, may become vague. Occupational ground rules, clearly spelled out, may assist in maintaining a proper balance between and within the double lives both are leading; i.e., marital and business.

There are possible advantages outside the family relationship. Social Security, workmen's compensation, even perchance, unemployment insurance, to name governmental aspects.

An employment contract between spouses should meet the standards of a similar contract between strangers, plus whatever leavening provisions are deemed desirable in their particular situation. A covenant to will the business to the survivor and their children might be on the agenda for consideration. Otherwise how will the employee-spouse be assured of a reward beyond wages?

Recordkeeping; taxes

Each family should maintain a log covering its business cruise. Here we are not speaking of a personal diary, which Mrs. Cady may have started in prep school days and continued indefinitely—if she dared to refrain from burning it before the wedding. Nor do I refer to the meticulous minutes which should be kept to record the decisions of the trustees of family trusts and the directors of family-owned corporations. Nor of the daily, monthly, and annual books of account of the family business or profession.

I have in mind something akin to all, but quite different. It is a log of the important business and financial decisions and programs of the family. It need not be a burden. Copies of income-tax returns reveal annual financial results. The checkbook traces spending and is not a bad diary. It recalls the trip to Europe and Jimmy's first long-pants suit and his expensive years at college.

The log I suggest, supplemented by the type of records just mentioned, is a notebook record of significant decisions and activities, revealing the compelling reasons for and perhaps some persuasive arguments against, a key decision which turned the family ship on a new course.

It will include the growing (we hope) annual balance sheets. It will serve as a record, preserving separate ownerships if thought desirable, or the merger of properties, if such is the path surveyed for the future. It will note oral advice given by lawyers and accountants in respect to family programs and incorporate their written opinions—often otherwise lost around the house, yet perhaps invaluable as a base point a decade later.

Within a closely knit family wherein family affairs are openly discussed, the log may be kept by a teen-ager. Such a family is less apt to fly apart.

The specter of taxes must never be forgotten when considering postnuptial agreements. A present or large gift from one spouse to the other may result in an immediate tax. By way of reminder, this will again be mentioned in the next chapter.

6

Estate Planning;
Trusts

The preceding chapter has mainly to do with varied business relationships between spouses, sometimes as though they were not married. It also touches upon contracts with outsiders. We now turn to family affairs, as such. There are a number of *intra* (within)–family relationships where a contract may be useful. A will comes at once to mind.

Wills

Not infrequently a situation develops in the evolution of the family when it becomes desirable to make certain that the will of one spouse, or those of both, contains specific provisions that cannot be changed without mutual written consent. Then parents will both know that their testamentary plans will be carried into effect and not be discarded by the survivor, regardless of the pleading of a new spouse. A contract freezing a will may be enforced by the person or persons for whose benefit it was made. He or she should know about it and, preferably, have a counterpart of it.

Assets earmarked for the care of a blind child would be one example of special provisions contained in a will. The funding of the cost of professional training for gifted children would be another. Absent a contractual obligation to keep it in force, a will is ambulatory, subject to change. A wife fears that she may be the first to pass away and that a subsequent marriage may change the viewpoint of the husband in respect to their present testamentary plan for their children, which they now agree is right. She may find great comfort in a contract committing both of them to that program. The husband may readily concur: "I am as interested in our children, love them as much as you do. I will agree that except for savings I generate *after* your death, all my property will pass to our children, just as now provided in our wills, unless we mutually agree to change the present plan. If I obligate myself to do this, so should you. Sometimes a widow in her sixties remarries and executes a new and completely different will."

A wife who is pressing for a formula freezing her husband's

will can scarcely object to that. So they enter into a contract pledging each other to provide for their children regardless of which spouse dies first. If old enough to be included in family financial discussions, the children should know of those mutual promises. That knowledge may eliminate a not unnatural monetary apprehension and soften the day-to-day relationships between the children and a not-too-welcome stepparent. It is important that an original of the agreement be available to them. If their other natural parent follows the first in death, they may have to bring suit to enforce the contract against a covetous now *former* stepfather or stepmother. Their own precursor who survived the first parental death having died, the relationship (though it is hoped friendly) with the transitory stepparent may be legally ended, unless there has been an adoption.

Depending on resources and circumstances, contracts making sure in respect to lesser testamentary provisions, whether of financial moment or merely emotionally important to one or both spouses, may bring peace of mind. One might reason as follows: "I know John will continue Mother's monthly allowance as long as he lives and is financially able to do so. But what if he should remarry, make a new will which ignores Mother, and then dies before she does? Or what if he gives my family heirlooms to a new wife?"

An integration—meaning harmony between the provisions of a prenuptial agreement, or one made during marriage, and both wills—is important. Conflicts between them invite controversy and perhaps litigation.

Most courts adhere quite closely to the view that when a different intention is not spelled out in the contract, the right of one spouse to inherit under the will of the other is not lost by a nuptial agreement or property settlement. As is the nature of nearly every general rule developed by the courts (called common law or decisional law), here and there is apt to be a statutory regulation to the contrary. As interpreted by the courts, the legislative enactment controls.

The desirability of contractual promises between husband

and wife when planning the disposition of their estates is not limited to the wealthy. If the assets of the first decedent are so great that the surviving spouse, their children, and dependent relatives, if any, will all receive ample largess on the *first* death, it does not matter greatly what the longer-living of the spouses does with his or her estate. It all may be devised and bequeathed to the church and charities, or pass, in part at least, to stepchildren acquired incident to a subsequent marriage, without really harming the issue of the prior marriage.

However, if family resources are limited, a binding agreement between the spouses as to disposition of all their properties, perhaps hard earned and saved together, may be indicated. Both will rest easier if they know that the accumulations of their lifetimes will reach their lineal descendants.

Life insurance should not be forgotten when discussing the transfer of property upon death. Most policies are apt to be on the life of the husband; upon his demise the proceeds may constitute a considerable or even a large proportion of his estate. If the wife wants assurance that after her death the proceeds of these policies will go to their children, the during-marriage contract should say so and the right of the husband, the insured, to change beneficiaries be deleted from the policies.

Merged families

The plethora of divorces has brought about an ever-increasing flood of second and subsequent marriages. When two families are to be merged by remarriage, the mother and father may feel the need of financial guidelines respecting the interests of the children charted in their prenuptial agreement (see "Prenuptial Agreements"). But more often than not, neither participant wishes to urge a practical prenuptial agreement. They may be as romantically foolish as at age eighteen. Or a contract may be discussed, and then neglected, or deliberately postponed until it be seen how the merged family melds. Or, as the children grow older and a fairer prediction can be made as to the future of each, the prenuptial agreement which seemed sound a decade ago may appear to be outmoded; it should be amended. The children have not developed as mother and father, the bride and groom of the second marriage, thought they would. Or the quips of fate may have dealt unevenly with the integrated offspring.

So it may be that, particularly with merged families, whether or not a prenuptial agreement was made, the time may come when a revised or a first during-marriage agreement should be consummated. This might be no more than disposition of properties after the death of one or both parents. Or it might have to do with financing some but not all of the children through college or helping one start in business, accompanied by formulas to equalize these *inter vivos* (during lifetime) advances. The remarried parents may promise to have equivalent extra largess in the wills for the benefit of the brothers and sisters, full or half, who did not share in the lifetime distribution or who received lesser amounts. The principal purpose of the contract may be to make immediate lifetime provision for a crippled child. If special arrangements are left in limbo, and the parents go out together in an automobile accident, there may be no special subsidy for the disabled child. After the sudden death of the parents, the child's siblings—whether full, step, or half—may prove strangely indifferent.

A firm written commitment by the wealthy second husband to provide for the wife's sickly child by her first husband might give that mother a consolation which would make a notable difference in family harmony and happiness. A lawyer may question legal enforceability, mumbling something about lack of consideration (pay for the promise). Depending on the circumstances of each family, some legal device can be adapted to the situation and make the protection substantially fail-safe.

Transfer of property; taxes; insurance

The specter of taxes must never be forgotten when consid-
ing agreements between spouses. A present gift may result
in an immediate gift tax. Prior to December 31, 1976, if the
deaths of the spouses and children occurred in anticipated
sequence, truly great savings could be made in estate and
inheritance taxes, particularly if there were a gift program
extending over a period of years. The Tax Reform Act of
1976 has greatly limited, but did not eliminate, the possibilities of saving taxes by careful planning. The advice of experts
will be necessary. Each situation must be examined within
its own framework. For these purposes the life insurance
program may be of paramount importance.

Trusts

A trust is a legal device which permits one person (the trustee) to hold title to property (the trust estate or trust property or *res*, meaning "the thing") for the benefit of another
or others (the beneficiary or beneficiaries). Under varying
circumstances it may be a most useful instrument for the
accomplishment of family objectives.

Trusts fall into two general categories. They are *inter vivos*
or testamentary. An *inter vivos* trust takes effect during the
lifetime of the trustor (the donor who established it). A
testamentary trust is part of a will and takes effect after the
death of the maker. In this study of marriage contracts, *inter
vivos* trusts are the primary interest. Also important are contracts between husband and wife to the effect that their wills,
or that of one of them, will contain a specified testamentary
trust.*

The family's *inter vivos* trust may be established by either
husband or wife, or both may join as trustors (grantors), the

* For more complete discussion of trusts, see Chapters VI and VII of *You
and Your Will by this author* (New York: McGraw-Hill, 1975).

title designating the persons who create the trust. Natural objectives impelling a husband and wife to favor and agree upon the formation of an *inter vivos* trust include:

a. Protection of themselves (the parents; the grandparents; whoever sets up the trust) during their lifetimes.

b. The education of children or contributions to educational institutions.

c. Provision for a disabled or incompetent child.

d. Protection of other members of the family or valued friend.

e. Creation or support of eleemosynary efforts—meaning a hospital, the performing arts, a museum or art gallery, or even a gift to the hometown for a statue of Great-Grandfather in the village square.

f. For religious activities, whether current income from the trust is to flow to the church or synagogue for operating expenses or to pay for a pipe organ or stained-glass window.

g. For any other good work where the Internal Revenue Service will recognize the gift as exempt from taxes.

Some of the foregoing trust objectives connote considerable wealth in the coffers of the trustors. Others do not. Because of financial hazards in their own affairs, a father and mother might agree to divest all their modest or even meager savings to some of the purposes listed and to insulate them from risk by a trust rather than keep the assets in their own names as individuals.

The law wisely authorizes specialized *inter vivos* trusts for the accomplishment of some of these objectives. A most admirable tool is called the Clifford Trust. It is adaptable to situations where the husband and wife, the trustors, wish to protect someone for at least ten years or for life of the beneficiary. When that purpose has been fulfilled, they may retrieve the then assets of the trust estate. Meanwhile the trust accomplishes two major purposes:

a. It takes care of the beneficiaries as instructed by the trustors.

b. It takes out of trustors' overall income whatever income would otherwise accrue to them from the properties (stocks, bonds, real estate, oil leases, anything) which they put into their Clifford Trust. The trust or beneficiary will be required to pay taxes measured on the income of the trust. But since usually the trust is established to protect someone of minimal income (such as an impoverished relative, a disabled person, or a student), the tax should be at a very low rate when contrasted with that of the husband and wife who agreed on the program and created the trust. *Caveat*: If the trust is established to educate minor children, it is advisable to have it funded by *grand*father and *grand*mother or a childless but loving aunt or uncle. The parents have a legal duty to support and educate the children and may not be given the benefit of the income-tax reduction.

Sometimes, after a few years, the husband and wife decide they do not want their property returned to them, or the survivor of them, when the trust terminates. They can then amend the trust and provide that it is to be distributed to their children or to a charity or to whomever they wish. Depending on who is to receive the funds when the trust purpose is accomplished, there may be an immediate gift tax. But that will not result in an increase in the aggregate of gift, estate, and inheritance taxes. Indeed, there may be some saving.

Power of attorney

As is implicit throughout, there are countless decisions and promises between husband and wife which meet all the judicial requisites of a contract, but no one would think of being so technical and stuffy as to put them in writing—"signed, sealed, and delivered." One spouse has an idea. It is proposed out of the blue, a complete surprise to the other. Or the plan evolves from discussion, perhaps over a long period of time. Finally they agree, then act.

It may be a trip to the Orient and around the world. They read the brochures and perhaps employ a travel agent to help work out the itinerary. Then come third-party contracts— with the travel agent or directly with the airlines and hotels. Those necessary contracts are between the prospective travelers and third parties, not *within* the family. But what about the agreement between themselves as to whose funds shall be drawn upon to pay the bills? Her separate funds? His, recently inherited? Savings from his current earnings?

Whatever the ultimate results, there will be either a gift from one to the other or an agreement as to how their odyssey should be financed. On the blackboard the law professor could diagram: (1) preliminary exploration of the project; (2) a definite offer: "If we fly first class, I will pay half from my inherited funds"; (3) acceptance and reliance on the offer —a fabulous trip. Nevertheless, upon return, the offeror ("I will pay half") reneges, and their joint savings bank funds from which the travel agent was paid and the American Express travel checks were purchased have been drained for the entire financing. Someone has broken a contract. The defense is "misunderstanding," and if it is a good marriage, the incident will be forgiven and forgotten, or nearly so. But later it may be resurrected as an example in a serious list of grievances.

A formal written contract designed to prevent a misunderstanding between the spouses in respect to charging the $10,000 expenditure would have seemed artificial, wholly unnecessary, a sign of distrust. But an imaginative spouse can see to it that a written record sufficient to preclude forgetting and consequent controversy be made unobtrusively in one of at least three ways, none so crass as a legal-looking paper starting with a "whereas" or two as though it had been dictated by a hackneyed lawyer: (1) prudently prepare a budget for the trip, naturally showing source of funds to meet the principal items; perhaps keep it with the mementos of the journey; (2) make a memorandum of the determinations, to be included as part of the recordkeeping (the family diary) advocated in the concluding part of the section "Agreements during Marriage"; (3) while preparing and packing for the trip, see to it that the big bills are all paid directly from the separate funds against which, by a then current agreement, they have been allocated.

The foregoing illustration tied to a journey brings out principles and procedures applicable to greater and more enduring affairs.

An agreement to buy a house might be an example. Whose funds shall pay for it and who shall hold title? There may be good reasons to have it in the wife's name alone. But, between them, should there be a writing so that the husband, or his successor, can prove his half interest in it? That might become important, regardless of who dies first.

Consider also the ownership of savings. Both spouses work. His salary is ample to support the family and pay the monthly installments of their house and car. She has habitually put all her earnings in savings banks in her own name or in their joint names *without* the right of survivorship, shortly reviewed. Should not the family archives contain a record clearly stating their agreement as to the ownership of her savings? At some point, such a testimony may be of great importance to heirs or creditors, or the parting spouses themselves, while negotiating a separation agreement. Or when trying to reach a compromise with a tax gatherer who claims all the savings should be taxed as part of the wife's estate.

The above comments apply in principle regardless of the type of investments held in her name. The essence may well be: Whose savings are they—hers, his, or theirs? What was the agreement in that regard? The question can arise when, in addition to keeping house, an alert and energetic wife develops a Gift Shoppe and invests her earnings in her own name. The husband has subsidized the shop by supporting her. The question here, and in analogous situations, is not what should the division be, but what do they want it to be? The suggestion is that there should be an unstilted, pleasant, written agreement between them to forestall later disputes between themselves or others, perhaps after both are gone. The preceding comments can apply to the allocation of household and all other expenses.

Passing reference was made to joint bank accounts. An agreement between husband and wife to have all or at least part of their funds in joint accounts is very common, and desirable. It is convenient for either to be able to sign checks. Usually the only contract they sign is the form furnished by the bank or savings institution. It is astonishing how often, particularly a few years later, neither spouse can remember (probably never really understood) what specie of joint account they have. They both remember signing; one thinks it was a pinkish 3 x 5 inch card and the other remembers blue. A phone call to the bank will elicit the desired information as to contents of the card, but meanwhile neither party knows:

    a. Whether the mutual authority to draw on the account terminates with the death of either.

    b. Whether it is a "survivorship account," with authority in the survivor of them to continue to withdraw funds.

    c. That the survivorship account controls over the disposition made by will.

    d. Between the two, who owns this asset?

If the mutual account or accounts aggregate a significant proportion of the family estate, a survivorship account may distort the testamentary plan of the real owner. Suppose, for example, a couple in their advanced years has relatively large sums in joint savings accounts, all with the right of survivorship. As a matter of convenience in the event of illness, they join their son who lives nearby as one of the depositors, with full survivorship withdrawal rights as stated on the bank cards.

The legal significance of those contracts never occurred to anyone, including the bank clerks who knew precious little beyond the fact that the blue card carried the mystical word *survivorship* and the pink did not.

Upon the death of both parents, all the joint account funds go to the son who had been made a joint depositor with the right of survivorship. He also shares one third each with his brother and sister in respect to the other assets of the parents which passed under the will. The question becomes: Will he act honorably and divide the savings one third each, as mother and father doubtless intended? Or will he insist on his legal rights and keep the bulk of the estate for himself? Obviously there should have been a contract among mother, father, and the son recording that if he should receive funds from the survivorship account, he would take them as a trustee, for the equal benefit of the three progeny. The other children should each have been given a copy of the document, or at least know of it and where a counterpart is safely lodged.

Akin to problems arising from joint accounts (all are easy of solution if attended to in advance) are those attendant upon issuance of securities in two names. That should not be done except upon the advice of counsel. Absent an agreement reciting ownership of the asset and assurance from counsel that regardless of which spouse dies first, the transmittal of the title will be confirmed or passed along in the most expeditious fashion, the husband and wife should not risk complicating their affairs by two-name securities. Usually, if bought with the wife's money, the certificate should be issued to "Mary Smith, in her separate estate"; if purchased with the family savings, in the name of the husband; if purchased with his separate funds, in the name of "John Smith, in his separate estate." An agreement may be useful, or clearly unnecessary, as counsel advises. An easily traceable source of separate funds, plus the instructions of the wills, may answer all questions. Or it all may have been taken care of in a sagacious prenuptial or during-marriage agreement. If there is no agreement, there may be uncertainty as to the ownership of assets, and genuine differences of opinion may fester into bitterness.

Third cousin to a joint account, but with far wider application, is a power of attorney. It is particularly useful as the spouses grow older and perhaps one has become incapable of handling business affairs. A power of attorney is a writing whereby a person constitutes another as his or her attorney (commonly called "attorney-in-fact") to serve in his or her place and stead. Until recently, following ancient law, the authority of the attorney-in-fact terminated with the death or mental incompetency of the grantor—the person who appointed someone as an attorney to substitute for him or her. This was logical enough. How, it may be asked, *if* a person is mentally incompetent to make business decisions (whether from illness, accident, or senility), how can it be known that as of *today* the grantor would want that particular person to be acting as his or her attorney-in-fact simply because some months or years ago that person was appointed? Now the rule is changing. In an increasing number of states, statutes permit a power of attorney to endure beyond the incapacity of the grantor if the intent is made clear.

This creates a most useful tool. An aging parent can constitute a convenient son, daughter, trusted friend, or relative as an attorney-in-fact, giving a nominee the power to continue even though senility or a more dreadful mental disorder should come to pass. Between husband and wife—running in either direction—it is a natural, if relative ages and health signal a go-ahead.

Then affairs can proceed without interruption. The expense and emotional discomfort to all the family of a guardianship proceeding in court will be avoided.

A power of attorney does not survive the death of the donor. If that stability is desired, as brought out earlier in this chapter, a trust is the appropriate legal mechanism.

Property
Settlement
and Separation
Agreements

1

The reader will have observed conflicts, or at least inconsistencies, between the rules pertaining to the *validity* of prenuptial contracts and contracts between spouses. Here is a good place to put them into perspective.

Validity

Rule 1. As previously stated in somewhat different language, assuming full disclosure and fairness, the courts encourage and uphold agreements between the prospective bride and groom and between spouses. The contracts are regarded as conducive to domestic tranquillity and the avoidance of controversy about the ownership, use, and inheritance of property.

Rule 2. Any contractual arrangement which substantially facilitates or encourages a divorce or separation is contrary to public policy and is void. The *Restatement of the Law* bluntly says, "A bargain to obtain a divorce or the effect of which is to facilitate a divorce is illegal." This is the traditional rule. But does not *every* prenuptial and during-marriage agreement which effectively disposes of property rights tend to make things easier if separation or divorce should come?

Rule 3. Facing realities, particularly in no-fault divorce states, courts and statutes now say that when their marriage contract faces fracture, a husband and wife have the capacity to execute a contract covering virtually every subject and incident of their relationship. Voluntary agreements of this nature are favored by the courts. Not long ago the Supreme Court of Illinois sanctified them, saying that a husband and wife on the verge of litigation or as parties to a divorce suit are to be commended for attempting to settle their interests amicably, because "this not only saves the court from being fraught with detail, and the necessity of repeated, recurrent hearings, but leads to better feelings and peace of mind."

Does not rule 3 conflict with rule 2 or is it not at very least an enormous exception to it? With variations, the new provisions of a typical no-fault divorce statute are to the effect that "in order to promote the amicable settlement of disputes attendant upon separation or divorce, husband and wife may enter into a written facilitating contract. It may provide for the maintenance of either of them, the disposition of any property owned by both or either of them and for the custody, support and visitation of their children and for the release of each other from all obligations except those stated in their contract." The new rule also applies to annulment proceedings.

Therefore, at this time, it must be said that in many states rule 2 has become outmoded when contending spouses are involved. Instead of being invalid because it facilitates divorce, a settlement agreement has become laudable because it eases dissolution.

I have not noticed a decision, though there may be one, which clearly carries the new doctrines back to prenuptial contracts and to agreements during marriage at a time when there is no conflict between the spouses. The new rules have not yet come all the way.

The practical answer is that every prenuptial agreement, and friendly contracts made during marriage, as well as property settlement and separation agreements, should be skillfully drawn. All three rules should be kept in mind in relation to the circumstances of the situation—whether warfare is present, probable, or merely possible.

What is said within the agreement, not the title the lawyer or the lawyer's secretary gives it, determines the nature of the contract. We will here examine the character and provisions of separation agreements, property-settlement agreements, and, a distinct variation, agreements to pay stated sums as or in lieu of alimony.

A separation agreement may be made without divorce in mind, at least for the present. At a minimum, it does contemplate that the couple will live separate and apart, permanently or for a trial period. The contract attempts to put their property affairs in order for that purpose. Often a separation agreement is a sensible first step if dissolution of the marriage is in the offing, and the separation agreement covers every subject which the parties can agree upon, thus shrinking to a minimum the areas of disagreement to be battled out in court. It is a combined property-settlement and separation agreement.

A diversionary query may occur to you. If the traditional rule is that an agreement to terminate a marriage is illegal, what about a contract *not* to marry? As in the case of covenants which facilitate divorce, the *Restatement of the Law of Contracts* gives a concise answer: "A bargain not to marry, or to be subject to loss or deprived of profit in case of marriage, or a bargain to hinder or prevent the marriage of another, is illegal, unless the bargain is otherwise reasonable and the restraint is incidental to another lawful purpose of the bargain." What would be "incidental to another lawful purpose of the bargain"? A mining company is considering employment of a geologist for a two-year stay in a remote area where it would be impracticable to take a spouse. Applicants for the job must be unmarried and agree not to marry before returning from the tour of duty abroad.

Agreements designed to be permanent

Prenuptial agreements look hopefully forward, anticipating a successful marriage. Separation agreements admit failure. Sometimes the adversaries remain friends; there are few recriminations. But all too often the agreement is a peace treaty, ending protracted conflict. Military men say that planning the strategy and tactics for retreating legions is more difficult than determining those of the force pressing forward.

In somewhat like fashion, a separation agreement spells out plans for retreat and surrender. It is between opponents, both of whom have lost. True, they may have reached the stage where an armistice seems clearly preferable to an open contest in court, perhaps exploited in the press and on the air. Both may almost gladly sign if the document is plainly drawn and fairly intended. However, fundamentally they are defeated spouses, each trying to salvage as much as possible.

Most separation and property agreements are, I suppose, designed to be permanent. If there are children or alimony or continuing involvements in property, the agreement is a working plan, not truly a final settlement. It does not assure an immediate end to all problems stemming from the marriage. The spouses (if not divorced) or the ex-spouses (if divorced) must still deal with each other, perhaps in varied fields for a long time. It takes a baby a score of years to become twenty-one. A principal objective of those who draft the agreement is to make it possible to cooperate harmoniously, with minimum acrimony.

In contrast, when there are no minor children and a dissolution of the marriage quickly follows the signing of the contract, accompanied by a prompt and final segregation of property, the book is closed except for mixed memories. This is particularly so for the ex-spouse who makes a happy subsequent marriage.

Recognizing that "permanent" settlement agreements are subject to abrogation by the formerly quarreling but recently reconciled spouses who hopefully reestablish their home and, if divorced, remarry each other, we will first discuss complete contracts and then turn to lesser arrangements.

A separation and property agreement which is designed to be permanent, whether or not divorce should come, will involve some and may include all the following subjects and perhaps more:

a. Disposition of property and income: Includes property acquired after marriage, as by inheritance.

b. Children: Custody and support. Visitation rights. Place of residence.

c. Periodic payments for support.

d. Family dependents: Subsidy to parents or others who have been receiving largess?

e. Adjustments as conditions change.

f. Effect of remarriage of ex-spouse or marriage of child.

g. Pensions; continuing life insurance.

h. Death of either: Possible commitment regarding one or both wills.

i. Funding by trust or other legal device.

j. Minimizing taxes: State and federal income taxes and all forms of death dues.

k. Living apart; no molestation; mutual releases.

l. Arbitration—what law governs?

m. Possibility of divorce (dissolution) proceedings.

n. Additional instruments; entire contract; notices.

We bypass the formal recitals—identification of participants, when and where married, residence, and other framework for the agreement—except to say that while the tone of the separation agreement can scarcely be as friendly, as loving, as the prenuptial agreements described in an earlier section, there is no need for animosities to show either in or between the lines. References may be naturally made to "husband" and "wife," rather than to "party of the first part" and "party of the second part," as though they were strangers. In short, the amanuensis should strive for as amicable a parchment as possible. Remember, there is an outside chance that they may be reconciled within a few weeks, half a dozen months, or even several years after signing! Sometimes embattled couples kiss and make up in the course of a bitter court trial.

Recitals designed to negate fraud or coercion are fashionable. These pious statements do no harm. In effect each asserts: "I have been honest in my representations. I was not coerced into signing this." The proof of the pudding is whether there actually have been frank and open dealings, one with the other. There should be—plus family records sequestered to prove the facts of complicated or delicate involvements. The spouses should have separate counsel.

Now we will briefly comment on the preceding fourteen-point checklist.

1. *Disposition of Property and Income.* Here we are talking of property, every kind of property. A complete inventory should be compiled. I do not imply that every small item should be listed, unless it has nostalgic value. But a set of sterling silver given by the parents of the *groom* might be treated differently than other wedding presents.

Agreed or appraised valuations should be assigned to significant items; though not necessarily mentioned in the contract, this is essential to the negotiations. What is the home worth? If there is a mortgage, or if it is being bought on contract, who assumes the liability? The one who is *not* to pay should remember that the rights of the creditor may not be affected by an agreement between the debtors. The spouse who crossed the mortgage note from his or her list of liabilities may still have to pay if the other spouse does not.

Valuations of listed securities and bank accounts pose no problems. But what of a risk investment in real estate, improved or unimproved, or partnership, and other interests where opinions as to value may differ greatly? If the spouses can not concur as to a fair value, an objective appraisal by disinterested experts may cost less than prolonged negotiations between the attorneys. Even a sole proprietorship where both have worked may be difficult to value when one is to keep it and the other is to take his or her share in dollars or other property. Already used as illustrations are: the neighborhood grocery, open when all else is closed, the proprietors living above or in back, with one almost always on duty; a dry-cleaning establishment; and a farm, not necessarily a small one.

These are family ventures where both contribute directly to operations. There are other proprietorships where the wife does not participate directly. Her contribution is that of mother and housewife. If the husband has partners, the settlement agreement should not complicate the business life of the former husband by a permanent ownership interest of a divorced wife. The contract should (1) recite the relative rights of husband and wife in jointly owned property and what is to be done with it and (2) dispose of all financial claims of each spouse against the other or against the other's property.

If the thwarted spouses can communicate, they should attempt to agree in principle on a fair division, then submit their tentative decision to the attorneys for refinement.

Property problems range from nothing except personal effects to large holdings of fluctuating or uncertain value. Timing may be important. The one immutable rule is to attempt to reach an equitable division within the perimeter of each factual situation. Probable earning power of the spouses may be an important factor: he is perpetually ill or is handicapped; she is strong and has an excellent job. They have no children. Should the wife receive half of a $100,000 aggregate? Should she help support him?

Usually it is not easy to reach a mutually satisfactory division unless the strife-ridden spouses are: (1) almost penniless, (2) so wealthy that each remains wealthy after the division, or (3) one or both have fundamental aspects of sainthood.

Income of course derives from one of two sources: (1) earnings and (2) the usufruct of property whether by way of dividends, interest, rents, and, perhaps, capital gains or other benefits. Often it would be a challenge to the wisdom of a Delphic oracle to reach a fair formula. Seemingly equitable today, it may be distorted by the time of the first anniversary of the contract.

A probability of property yet to come poses problems. Suppose that one of the contestants is likely to inherit considerable wealth. Or that their grazing land is subject to an exploration lease to Union Oil. They just might tap a gusher! Should the spouse who takes the grazing land, or part of it, as his or her share of the marital assets, enjoy all oil royalties? The possibility of receiving relatively large amounts of property after the divorce should not be ignored when compiling the family inventory.

2. *Children.* When a contending couple stands at the bar of justice for a determination of the custody, support, and visiting rights of children, the objective of the judge will be to do what is best for each child. The wishes, often rivalries, of the parents will be secondary—distinctly secondary. Children who are old enough to have a cogent viewpoint will probably be given a chance to state it. Sometimes a wise and kindly judge will talk to a child alone in chambers, insulated from parents, attorneys, courtroom personnel, and visitors.

Usually young children are entrusted to the mother, but not always; she may be manifestly unfit. Often, if not usually, the recommendations of older, stable-appearing children will be followed. But at best it is a contest, often resulting in greater bitterness than the worst haggling over property and alimony.

If at all possible, the parents should reach an agreement respecting the support of the children, custody (which may be a burden as well as a joy), educational programs, visitation prerogatives, and all other matters which may be important to the children.

Whatever they decide will be subject to review and change by the court. The compromise reached by bitter, bickering parents may not appeal to the judge as in the best interests of the children.

It is highly desirable that a settlement agreement contain indicia of a program for the children which, as of the moment, seems the best *attainable*—not merely *obtainable* through negotiations between distraught parents and attorneys who will try to please their clients.

The agreement should realistically recognize the possibility of radical change, particularly if the children are small. Two girls are entrusted to the mother. What if she is subjected to a long period of illness? Or assume that the father prospers and his income is sharply up. Should his former wife continue to work if she is needed at home to care for a frail child? The countless contingencies of life cannot be foretold and cataloged. But hard as it is to do, the general policies of a long-range plan for the children should be spelled out. Does "schooling" end with high school, college, or professional school? Is the father bound to pay for a child's expensive training in music or painting? He has slight appreciation of any of the arts; he believes himself to be a practical man.

Should the divorcée be allowed to whisk the children to another (perhaps distant) state where her new husband's work is located? Or if she is working and can secure a much better job across the Alleghenies or Rockies? Are not the father's rights to see his children frequently as important as a larger paycheck for the divorced mother?

There will be no crystal ball to foretell the vicissitudes of life. The gist is that the best possible program should be planned for the children, irrespective of the real or passing desires of the parents. And it should be reemphasized that the welfare of a growing child may require drastic modification of plans which once looked best but have become outmoded.

3. *Periodic Payments for Support.* These payments may be from husband to wife or from wife to husband. If a broad property-settlement agreement is being negotiated and a formula for periodic payments in lieu of alimony is on the agenda, it is natural to combine the end results in one instrument. But since alimony, looking only to the future, is at least theoretically a thing apart from a settlement of rights in presently existing assets, it will be discussed under a separate heading.

4. *Family Dependents.* Not all impoverished mothers-in-law are irritants. Some are loved and revered. Or perhaps the habit of a well-placed couple has been to send the wife's venerable Uncle Arthur a check for $50 each month; it is the money margin which makes a livable world for him.

Such situations where a prosperous spouse would elect to carry on are not numerous. The mere possibility is mentioned here, as on a checklist. In some instances, a provision in respect to dependents (other than children) should not be a covenant to pay; it may be a mere statement of a present revocable intent to do so.

5. *Adjustments as Conditions Change.* When circumstances permit a clear-cut division of property (no support money for children and no alimony), the financial book is closed. But, except for short, youthful marriages which end before the first car has been paid for, at least a modicum of continuing financial relationship is not unlikely.

It may become extremely important to the obligor (the spouse upon whom the future payments fall) that the settlement agreement include recognition of the possibility of change, down as well as up. A formula for periodic payments may seem and be fair enough as of the day of signing. But fate may have decreed great changes in need or ability to pay. Because of economic factors wholly beyond his or her control, the income of the former spouse may plummet. Or because of the illness of the ex-spouse or children, their needs may sharply increase. Often the courts have power to adjust payments to meet the new realities. But it is well to recognize in advance that the father, a physician who was confident of his ability to finance his two sons through medical school, may find himself a patient and be unable to practice full time. Here, it will have been noticed, the emphasis is on change in the fiscal situation of parents, in contrast to needs of children stressed under point (2).

Incidentally, when one spouse honestly thinks the agreement calls for far too much money and the other wails that it is unfairly low, it is likely that the scales balance fairly evenly.

6. *Effect of Remarriage of Ex-spouse or Marriage of Child.* A remarriage of either ex-spouse may become important in two principal areas: finances and custody of children.

The money aspect will be considered shortly when discussing alimony. Except when the departing husband cannily encourages remarriage by continuing the subsidy, or part of it, for a stated period, alimony as such usually ends when the wedding bells peal again. That would not be true for an incompleted division of property, unless so stated in the separation agreement.

Upon remarriage of either ex-spouse, the situation in respect to custody of children may change fundamentally. Assume a divorce, two young children, and a father whose income is barely sufficient to support a united family of four, much less a divided family—two establishments. He is a considerate and loving father; his only real problem is low earning capacity. The divorced wife must seek a job; no longer will she be able to welcome the two kiddies home from school with the smell of fresh cookies in the kitchen. Seeking her share of gaiety, many evenings she leaves them at home alone.

The pleasant but financially deficient fellow whom she divorced is found attractive by a widow who adores children, including his. Her deceased husband left her lush in funds. She is eager for a new family, including the two children. Should there be a change in custody? An occasional divorcée mother might welcome it. For most, a change in custody would bring anguish, perhaps greater than did the divorce itself. There may be no easy or even comfortable solution for a divorced mother who loves her children.

These illustrations do *not* suggest that all the possible ramifications of a remarriage and the effect upon the children can be foreseen and covered by contract. Not even when a remarriage to a known person is contemplated at the time the settlement agreement is negotiated. As long as there are minor children, the possibility of the need of change is present.

When children become of legal age or marry, they are considered emancipated. The legal duty of the parents to provide financially is usually ended. But often that is not the answer. Parents may wish to subsidize the completion of an educational program, even though not obligated to do so. Each situation must be decided on its own—parental resources and wishes vis-à-vis current performance and potentials of the progeny.

7. *Pensions; Continuing Life Insurance.* With increasing frequency, a pension is possible, probable, or certain for one or for both of the parties. It may be called retirement pay. The terms of the contract with the employer may be important to the settlement agreement. A spouse may have an already vested (owned) interest in a fund, and the present value of each participant's share may be subject to calculation. Or it may all be subject to tenure on the job. There may be provisions pertaining to partial assignments. In short, the attorneys should check coming pensions and retirement pay.

Sometimes life insurance is forgotten in a marriage settlement. Or, if remembered, proper checks are not established to assure payment of premiums before due date, with time for the beneficiary to make the payment if necessary to prevent cancellation. Perhaps the insured is no longer insurable under a new policy.

Emotionally it may be easier for the insured divorced father to pay substantial premiums for insurance upon his life if the proceeds are earmarked (perhaps through a trust) for the education of his children. If he lives until all are through school (define "school") or when the youngest reaches, say, age twenty-two, the policy reverts to him. Suppose three children and three policies, each $15,000. As each graduates from college or becomes twenty-two, whichever first occurs, the ownership of that child's policy returns to the father.

The target of this illustration is to suggest that a divorced husband might willingly covenant to carry much more insurance for the benefit of his children with reversion rights to him upon named events, including death of a child, than he would carry for the benefit of a divorced wife and, through her, possibly for the dollar advantage of her next husband.

8. *Death of Either.* The death of either may seem utterly remote to those who hit marital snags early in life. If there are no children, perhaps the grim specter may be disregarded.

Or perhaps not. It might make full performance of the property-settlement aspect of their contract either unnecessary or impossible. Protection through life insurance has already been listed.

Here is an illustration beyond things monetary: If the ailing divorced wife and children are expected to live with the doting maternal grandparents, should the contract be silent as to whether the children will be transferred to their father or stay in their then accustomed home with the older generation in the event of the death of the divorced wife?

Perhaps the contract should not speak explicitly on this subject. Or perhaps it should. All that can be said here is that the effect of death should not be ignored by inadvertence.

Though appropriate occasions are infrequent, a commitment in regard to the will of one or both of the spouses may be worth exploring as a tool in reaching an equitable overall formula. In any event, the contract should either surrender or spell out the rights of each upon the death of the other.

9. *Funding by Trust or Other Legal Device.* Occasionally there is a situation where it is advantageous to fund the obligations of the divorcing husband or wife. For the sake of her children (she of course having custody), a wealthy wife might want to be sure that the alcoholic whom she is divorcing will have enough to live on and appear in respectable raiment when visiting his offspring. Her attorney might advise the establishment of a trust which would send him a monthly allowance. Upon his death, the fund would be for the benefit of the children and perhaps their children if he lived long enough. Monthly payments might be dependent upon a semblance of sobriety.

There are many variations in methods of funding which, in some situations, are worth exploring. Whatever is done should be carefully tailored. This sort of a garment cannot be bought off the rack.

10. *Minimizing Taxes.* The impact of taxes has scarcely been mentioned as we strode briskly through the foregoing

checklist. In wealthy families, the tax impact might be severe. The promises of the contract should be such and couched in language such that taxes are minimized; that is for the benefit of all concerned.

If the income of the divorcing husband is likely to greatly exceed that of the coming divorcée, certainly the settlement agreement should be kept within the rules whereby she pays the taxes measured by income upon payments received from him. Conceivably, this alimony payment might even be higher, yet no greater burden on the husband. These are technical matters, and both parties should have the benefit of the advice of counsel well grounded in tax aspects plus, if thought desirable, the viewpoint, calculations, and projections of a skilled accountant.

11. *Living Apart; No Molestation; Mutual Releases.* The contractual coverage of physical separation may be for a limited period, as an experiment, or forever. No matter how clearly spelled out, circumstances may bring them together, perhaps beside the bed of a sick child or at a large neighborhood Christmas party they have both habitually attended. After a few Tom and Jerrys, most anything may happen.

If the wife has the slightest apprehension, the contract should contain an appropriate commitment from the husband not to intrude himself upon her and the children. Visitations and periods when the children are to be with him may be scheduled.

If the contract purports to be literally a *complete* settlement of their affairs (it rarely is), it should include mutual releases.

12. *Arbitration—What Law Governs?* It has been stressed that *except* when within a most simple framework (no minor children; no, or a specified, period of alimony; property, if any, easily divisible) a settlement agreement does not spell *finis est*. Rather it is in the nature of an operating agreement; not infrequently prolonged. Sharp differences may arise despite good-faith efforts on the part of both to

perform properly. And, of course, there may be deliberate evasion by either party or both. In such tragic event, almost inevitably the court is the forum.

When there are sincere misunderstandings which cannot be resolved by discussion, an arbitration clause, spelled out in the contract, may prove useful. Perhaps the parties and counsel will be satisfied with submission to the American Arbitration Association—usually expeditious but relatively expensive.

But here the contestants may be submitting family matters to strangers who have far less experience than full-time judges wearing black robes to depersonalize themselves as people prying into others' troubles.

If an arbitration clause is deemed constructive, I would prefer a formula tailored to the needs of the family. The very best nominees for arbitrators may not be on the rolls of the Arbitration Association. If counsel representing the parties both believe an arbitration clause desirable, they will have suggestions as to how it should be worded.

Usually, but certainly not inevitably, it is plain what law governs. It will be that of the state wherein the fragmenting family has been living. But perhaps before the agreement, the husband and wife went their different ways and already live in different states. Or possibly they have been so itinerant that their domicile is uncertain. Counsel may agree that for legal reasons one possible state is better than the other. When the question "What law governs?" cannot be answered with absolute certainty, it should be stated in the contract.

13. *Possibility of Divorce (Dissolution) Proceedings.* It has been noted that in some states a settlement agreement may be held invalid if the objective is to facilitate or secure a divorce. There the theory and tone of the contract should be: "If divorce proceedings should ensue, we will recommend this agreement to the court for approval and adoption." The traditional hypothesis is that spouses may not conclusively agree to have a divorce because the sovereign state has a paramount interest in the marital status. Hence it cannot be

terminated without the permission of the court. However, it has been seen that in respect to dissolution of marriages, the law is in a period of flux. Counsel advising in respect to the settlement agreement will know what can safely be said, or should not be said, in a particular jurisdiction, in light of the most recent legislative or judicial guess as to what social policy should be.

14. *Additional Instruments; Entire Contract; Notices.* Except in those fortunate instances where there is truly a windup as a phase of executing the documents, the paper should include a legend to the effect that both will provide such further documents as may be necessary or convenient to effect the purpose of their treaty. A deed, a bill of sale covering the Buick, and other instruments may be overlooked or the signing naturally come later. Take as an example a note to the bank. He has assumed the obligation. But the bank will not let her off, and she painfully must sign renewal notes until the debt is paid, perhaps partly from the earnings or property of his next wife.

If the settlement agreement is intended to be complete, it should so state. It is their entire peace treaty, meaning that there are no unwritten arrangements of any importance and that one may not put legal pressure on the other based on a fancied oral promise.

Here are two kinds of notices—one to each other and another of different wording to third parties. The first is easy. Merely say where notices shall be sent, subject to change when one of them moves. Written notices may be required for certain types of communication.

The second kind of notice may be difficult to agree upon. The wife's purse rattles with plastic credit cards, and she has a few open accounts. The husband asserts that her spending proclivities are a principal cause of their estrangement. If there is not to be an immediate divorce, with consequent notice to all the world, what notice should be sent? The husband hopes he can trust her to close every charge account now in his name and hers and to open none wherein the creditor has any right to look to him. Or perhaps the working or affluent wife feels she needs protection against bills incurred by her departing husband at one of his clubs or taverns.

The possible desirability of advising creditors, present and potential, should not be missed. It need not be done with unnecessarily abrasive vigor.

Obviously the foregoing fourteen factors could be separated into a hundred. Indeed, already there has been considerable subdivision in the course of discussion.

Here the caveat must be that no inventory of possible points can honestly purport to be complete. Deliberations incident to deciding on terms and terminology may bring a new facet to mind, not yet before a court or mentioned in a law book. Such is the nature of human relationships.

But a review of the problems and possibilities enumerated above should suggest almost everything which it is possible to foresee.

Separation with hope of reunion

Temporary separation agreements range from type 1, an informal oral or written arrangement to live apart for a designated period while minds are being made up, to type 2, a comprehensive signed separation agreement which will become legally effective at the end of the trial run *unless* meanwhile there is a reconciliation.

This checklist may be exceedingly short. If the separation is pure type 1, little more is needed than a stipulation providing for the expenses of the nonworker, care of the home, children, and pets, and the miscellanea which become important when one goes on a long trip. Possibly both are employed and neither will leave town. It is hoped that not-unpleasant living arrangements can be found for each. Sometimes they "separate" but continue to live in the same building—formerly a home, now merely a house!

If the "temporary" separation is type 2, the fundamental agreement to which the trial period relates should be polished with the care which would be given it if it were to be effective and final as of the day of signing—with no wait-and-see period.

Or there can be hybrids—some things determined; others left open until the separation experiment has ended. This interim agreement would not contain the recital that it comprehends their entire contract.

So for your checklist for a temporary agreement, merely study the items which should be thought of when entering into a complete permanent agreement. Develop only those you wish for this temporary purpose, knowing that if reconciliation fails, negotiations must begin in earnest.

Then, of course, there are the variations based on the calendar. Assume a husband past retirement age enjoys a handsome corporate pension but, having lived extravagantly (wife may have been the spender!), so little property has been accumulated that they lack earning assets to divide. Perhaps this elderly divorcée is entitled to alimony for life, including a charge against whatever estate he leaves.

With women's status in the economy (professional, business, industrial) moving upward, the trend is to treat the disillusioned parties as equals. No longer is the wife indubitably a helpless homemaker, mistreated by a ruthless husband. Unless willing and financially able to pay a fancy price for freedom, in the absence of a special situation, the parting settlement agreement should keep alimony to a minimum, or (subject to an adjustment period) eliminate it altogether *if* (but only if) the age and training of the wife put her in the earning segment of society. But suppose they married when he was twenty-four and she was twenty. Now fifty, she has had no business experience; she has devoted herself to the home, her husband, and their children and (during the last few years) to nursing grandchildren through periods of childhood ailments plus special care of the little boy who is disabled.

Should she not receive alimony for life, backed by a claim

against the estate of her former husband in the event of his death?

Alimony

As it is popularly understood, the term "alimony" means the obligation of a divorced husband to make periodic payments to his former wife. It traces to the Latin *alimonia* meaning "nourishment, sustenance." A common differentiation is "support money" for the children; "alimony" for the wife. Sometimes they can be sharply segregated; sometimes not.

Alimony for the life of the wife—or at least until remarriage —followed naturally from the dual concept of the indissolubility of marriage and the ownership of all the property of the two by the husband. Since he owned everything, surely he must provide a living for her for life!

While we think of alimony as running from man to woman, historically that is not necessarily so. It may be defined as a fixed compensation to either spouse for the disruption of the marriage. Assume a wife, blessed with health and wealth. Her husband is incapacitated, without funds, and the prognosis is that he will never be able to support himself. Then the flow should be reversed and the alimony run from her to him.

In some early civilizations, the husband's unlimited right of divorce could be ameliorated by prenuptial alimony contracts. Indeed, some Greek states went the limit; they declared a marriage null and void if not bolstered by a property settlement for the wife in the event the husband (as was his right) decided to dispose of her.

The simple contemporary case is, of course, a relatively young divorcée, no children, with earning capacity or independent assets sufficient for her needs—if not all her wants. Then excessive judicially imposed alimony would be punitive, punishment visited upon the former husband. But if there are three or four children to be mothered, she may need alimony plus support money for the children until the children are on their own and she has been trained or retrained to support herself. In occasional circumstances a wife argues for, and the court grants, alimony for life (plus a claim against the estate of a deceased former husband) or until her remarriage. In a number of states, remarriage automatically terminates alimony unless the former partners have expressly agreed to the contrary.

A sharp cutoff of alimony on the date of remarriage may discourage the wife from another romantic venture. A far-sighted husband, faced with the inevitability of substantial long-term alimony, might think it prudent to encourage her subsequent marriage by letting the alimony run for a while after she remarries—perhaps in a reduced amount. She would, so to speak, have an installment dowry as an incentive to prospective suitors and be sooner off the payroll of the prior husband.

With this briefest background, we turn to a new world. Both spouses may be earners—she the better of the two. Or within a period measured in months or at worst not longer than two or three years, most younger women can absorb training sufficient to provide for themselves. Here we are assuming no small children.

So it is that after a fair division of property and provision for the children, both spouses are entitled to believe that their settlement agreement should *not* provide for permanent alimony, either he to her or she to him, except under special circumstances. Vocational education for the wife has just been mentioned. The current of alimony might run the other way. The husband, a structural worker, fell from a girder. Perhaps his ex-wife should pay him alimony for a limited period to supplement his workmen's compensation check while he learns a new trade.

Keeping alimony to a minimum is not inconsistent with the flexibility necessary or desirable in meeting unusual conditions. A recent New York decision furnishes a vivid example.

They were married while he was a third-year prelaw student at the University of North Carolina. She was a sophomore studying biology at Florida State University. Their plan was that he finish his undergraduate and law school education while she toiled. She did work, except for time off to have a child, until the marriage collapsed five years later. She was well able to support herself as a secretary.

The husband had a good job with a Wall Street law firm. The wife wanted to complete her medical education and become a doctor; she would not be a "drone" living on alimony. She would work during vacations. The court allowed her $200 a week for alimony and child support while a full-time student, taking prescribed premedical and medical courses. Remarriage would terminate the alimony (for her) portion of the award, with appropriate support money for the child to be continued.

Here, instead of meaning merely "nourishment" money, alimony includes funds for training to the wife's highest level of competency, which had been delayed while she supported her husband during his educational period.

A discussion of alimony would not be complete without emphatic reference to age as an important factor. (Relative health has already been mentioned.) Rarely would the untrained, middle-aged woman without an inclination toward business find it possible to locate a satisfying position. In the absence of a physical or mental breakdown, the husband has ten to fifteen good earning years ahead and then a pension plus his Social Security. Should she not receive a livable amount of alimony for life carrying with it a claim against his estate if he should predecease her?

8

Postdissolution
Contracts

There are three areas wherein the former spouses may find it advantageous to agree on changes in the pattern or rights, duties, and even ownerships as they were delineated when the decree of divorce was signed and entered by the court. They are (1) custody and support of the children, (2) alimony, and (3) property rights and obligations. Despite the adjudication memorialized in the decree of divorce or order of dissolution, the divorce court retains what is often called "continuing jurisdiction" in respect to items 1 and 2. Whatever should and can be done for the manifest benefit of the children will be done. As conditions change, alimony is usually subject to adjustment, up or down, as the former spouses themselves agree or the court itself determines. With property rights and obligations, the answer is the opposite. The judge may lack power to tamper with the determinations made in the divorce proceedings, particularly when based on a contract between the parties, or the judge may refuse to do so.

The three arenas will be examined serially.

Custody and support of children

Whether under express authority enacted in statutory form or because of its inherent powers, in most states, the divorce courts retain a continuing power to modify provisions in respect to the custody and maintenance of minor children. The authority of the court persists even though the divorce decree did not reserve it. An order of modification may itself be modified. Accordingly it is proverbial that, as to minor children, in a very real sense an order or decree of a divorce court is not final; it is subject to amendment for the benefit of the child so long as he or she is a minor. Lawyers have a name for it. As to children, the nature of the decree is "interlocutory."

When deciding whether to modify the mandates of the decree in respect to custody or control of a child, the court attempts to be guided by the fundamental precept that the welfare of the child is the primary concern. The original determination will not be altered unless the judge believes it will benefit the child. The test is the child's welfare, not that of either parent, or of both of them.

With the background of these judicial objectives, as to children, the parents are in somewhat the same position after divorce as they were before. If they cannot themselves agree upon changes relating to the children, including support money, upon petition of either of them the court will listen to both their stories, consider the testimony of witnesses brought in to bolster the viewpoints of the battling ex-spouses, and make its own decision, possibly anathema to both. Thus it becomes highly advantageous for the parents as well as the older children to realize that they are subjects of legal controversy (perhaps pictures and stories in the newspapers and over TV) if the parents cannot reach an accord. This may be several years subsequent to the divorce, after both have remarried.

As they are bargaining regarding changes, the former spouses should have in mind that they are still subject to the jurisdiction of the divorce court and that the judge will examine their modification proposals against guideposts such as these:

a. Have there actually been substantial changes in circumstances which have affected the child adversely or are likely to be harmful in the future? Has inflation had a damaging impact—more dollars for the money-maker but less purchasing power to support the child?

b. A change in custody is not in order merely because there has been great improvement in the financial position of the parent who pays support money for the child, enabling him or her to provide a more attractive home than the parent who has custody. Instead, the allowance for the child may be increased.

c. A change in the physical or mental health of the parent who has custody might clearly compel a change.

d. The same comment would apply if the custodian parent should become transient, no longer constantly available to care for the child. The itinerant way of life might be for good cause, as a job requirement, or attendant upon frivolous adventure. Regardless of cause, there is no parent at home; the child is entitled to have one if available.

e. Remarriage of a parent may or may not result in such a radical change in conditions that custody should be changed. Here the character and attitude of the step-parent might be significant or even of controlling importance.

f. Has the parent who has custody attempted to alienate the affections of the child from the other parent, or encouraged or permitted others to do so?

g. Has the parent who was originally denied custody because found unfit now been so restored physically, mentally, or morally that custody should be changed or divided? Should the children now be with the other spouse during vacations?

h. The question of financial support may intermingle with custody.

The fact that prior to divorce the parents made a contract covering custody and support of the children and the court incorporated it in the divorce decree does not affect the power of the court to modify the decree and, incidentally, their original stipulations.

And so it is that after divorce the situation in respect to reaching an agreement regarding children does not differ fundamentally from that which existed prior to divorce. If the parents can compose their differences, the judge will be apt to follow their recommendations. If they submit their contentions to him in a knockdown, drag-out court contest, he may decide on a formula unacceptable to the parents, but to which they must acquiesce.

A fairly drawn amendatory contract with the welfare of each child in mind is the best solution.

Agreements to modify alimony

The original concept of alimony has already been described. Family property was once vested in the husband, the lord and master of the hapless wife. Our jurisprudence is not the first to accord the wife her just dues. In many respects, as to things material, Islam was ahead of us, the harem notwithstanding. The property rights of wives were recognized.

Formerly, alimony for the wife was a necessity; her earning capabilities were probably low or nonexistent. Unless, as some court opinions have remarked, she took to the streets, she had no way to earn an adequate income. Naturally, under such conditions, a sustenance allowance for life or until remarriage was a part of the social and legal pattern.

Comparative financial resources are prime factors. This is so whether alimony is fixed by an agreement readily confirmed by the judge or determined by the court after hearing the contentions of the spouses and considering all relevant evidence introduced at the trial. Certainly a wife wealthy in her own right should not be allowed alimony if she discards a husband whose earning capacity is miniscule, despite his best efforts. Perhaps he should receive some!

If relative resources and need are fundamentals when first deciding on the amount and duration of alimony, it follows that allocations for alimony should not be inflexible, and should be subject to adjustment if radical changes in conditions should occur. This has already been mentioned. It is repeated as a foundation for the proposition that even after dissolution of the marriage, with an alimony formula spelled out in the decree, the former spouses should be willing to discuss and, it is hoped, reach an agreement regarding an amendment of the alimony formula, if and when drastic changes in the situation of either should occur. If her own income should be cut in half, an ex-wife whose earnings were in the order of $1500 a month when the divorce decree was entered cannot be expected to continue to mail a $400 check twelve times a year to her former husband to help pay his expenses at a tuberculosis sanitarium in Arizona. The ultimate question may be: Will they regretfully reach a compromise or will they fight it out in court, at a cost utterly disproportionate to the gap between them.

To summarize, responsive to the need in varied circumstances, by statute or inherent power, most courts may adjust and readjust alimony payments. As in the case of provisions touching minor children, the former spouses should attempt to agree in respect to realistic modifications of alimony schedules. Unless the divorce comes after the wife has lost her earning capabilities and the husband is well situated, the divorcing wife can no longer assume that the court will grant her alimony for the rest of her days. But certainly she should not be forced to spend them in penury if the former husband is favored with even modest financial resources.

Property rights and obligations

In contrast to matters affecting the welfare of children or alimony, the courts rarely tamper with (1) a property-settlement agreement which has received court approval or (2) a court adjudication of property rights and obligations. In many states, the court lacks authority to do so regardless of the merits. So the former spouses are almost always on their own as far as post-divorce modification of purely property matters is concerned, unless their contract or the decree provides for changes in order to accommodate to new conditions. All the parties can do is to bargain concerning altering then existing rights and duties in the hope of reaching a compromise.

That does *not* mean that because the court will not or cannot itself amend their contract or the decree, the parties should not do so. Perhaps the one favored by the status quo may be justified in taking a rigid position and adhering to a no. Or perhaps he or she is not.

For example: Their important, almost sole, investment is a machine shop which, as a going business, is worth $350,000.

The liquid assets are minimal. Earnings not funneled to taxes and support of the family have been devoted to the purchase of equipment. The big new lathe and new drill press are both being purchased on an installment plan. The property-settlement agreement and decree both provide for: (1) allocation of $175,000 to the wife by payment of the sum of $10,000 a year plus interest at 6 percent per annum on diminishing balances, with accelerated payments at husband's option; (2) security to the wife by a lien against the business until the $175,000 and interest be paid; and (3) alimony to the wife, $400 a month for three years or until her death or remarriage, if either should sooner occur. She remarries a year after the divorce, thus terminating alimony.

Two annual installments of $10,000, plus interest, had been made when came a major economic recession. The shop's best customer became bankrupt; no more orders would come from him, and payment for a large aggregate of prior deliveries would be through the trustee in bankruptcy at a rate of an estimated twenty cents on the dollar.

The former husband simply does not enjoy a cash flow sufficient to divert $10,000 a year plus 6 percent on $155,000 to the wife. It is hoped that the business will struggle through the crisis, as it has done before, and in a few years again return a good profit.

Although not obliged to do so, would it not be to the advantage of the former wife to consent to a new schedule of payments, attainable by the divorced husband and furnishing an incentive to him to carry on? If he should give up, the business would be worth little more than the salvage value of machinery and equipment, less obligations.

This book may read like a panegyric to good contracts as one of the solutions of family problems. It may well be. There is a superlative volume by Harry Scherman entitled *The Promises Men Live By,** 481 big pages. The author

*Published by Random House, New York, in 1938.

examines the role of promises in modern civilization, going back into history enough to include "What the Record Shows about Three Thousand Years of Fraud." He demonstrates the economic and political effect of the broken promises of rulers. He proves beyond doubt that promises which can be relied upon are essential through all ranges of activity—economic, political, social. This extends up to and includes the great powers whose vital promises made each to the other are recorded in documents usually called treaties. Without contracts there would be perpetual chaos at all levels of life.

Here we have examined the legal effect of the most important personal promises one can make—those attendant upon the creation and fulfillments of the marital and extramarital relationships. Family life is dependent on contract—reciprocal promises. This is true whether the subject of inquiry be a usual family or those relatively few skeptical sophisticates who believe themselves to be beyond the need of formal ties.

Just as Scherman pictured and assessed the place of promises in civilization as a whole, I have tried to describe the place of legally recognized promises in the operation of the basic unit of society, the family, whether in or out of wedlock. I hope this scrutiny of legal structure and possibilities may make this unit of civilization more nearly understandable and, for many, more workable, more durable and successful—therefore, happier.

Index

Additional instruments in
agreements, 29, 123
Agreements during marriage,
80–81
employment and, 89
extraordinary expenditures
and, 80, 101
household and, 80
joint bank accounts and,
103
joint venture and, 88
loans and, 82–85
ownership and, 80–81, 102
partnerships and, 86, 87
Alienation of affections, 10–11
Alimony, 125–128
age, as factor of, 128

Alimony (*Cont.*):
agreements to modify, 133
Social Security and, 128
Amendments:
child custody and support,
130
money-obligations, 134
property-rights, 134
Annulment, 54–55
Antenuptial contracts, 22, 54
(*See also* Prenuptial
agreements)
Arbitration, 121–122

Bank accounts, 102
joint, 103–104

Banns, 4
Betrothal, 1
  and the church, 5
  eligibility for, 8
Breach of promise, 9–10
  damages awarded for,
    11–14
  defenses against, 13
  presents and, 14–15
  proof of, 13–14

Children, 115–116
  (*See also* Property settle-
    ment and separation
    agreements)
Church, the, and betrothal,
  5
Common-law marriage, 5, 6
Competency to enter into
    prenuptial agreements, 34
Consortium, 48–49

Divorce, 51–56
  dissolution, concept of, 53
  no-fault, 55–59
Durant, Ariel, 3
Durant, Will, 3
During-marriage agreements
    (*see* Agreements during
    marriage)

Earnings, 27, 125
  during advancing years, 125
Edward VI, 2
Employment agreement, not
    betrothal, 41–42

Estate planning, 94–100
  trusts in, 98

Fiduciary relationships, 6
Filiation suits, 18
Fornication and the law, 63
Frauds, statute of, 4

Gifts (*see* Presents)
Good faith, 6–8
  previous marriage and, 8

Hazards in quasi- and same-
    sex marriages, 64–66
Heart-balm suits, 9–10
  (*See also* Breach of
    promise)
Henry VIII, 2
Heterosexual arrangements, 67
  children in, 71
  and home purchase, 65
  job problems in, 71
  and property ownership on
    death or dissolution, 67
  and public affairs, 66
Heterosexual legal solution(s),
  69–70
  cooperative enterprise as, 70
  joint ownerships as, 70
  partnerships as, 70
  trust relationships as, 69
  wills as, 71
Homosexuals, 64
  legality of marriage be-
    tween, 63, 72, 75
  legality of other contracts
    between, 76, 77

Insurance, life, 28, 98, 119

Joint bank accounts, 103–104
Joint venture, 87
Jurisdiction as influence on
     divorce proceedings, 122

Life insurance, 28, 98, 119

Marriage contracts, 46–60
     defined, 62
     inherent obligations in, 48
     termination of, 51
Mary, Queen of Scots, 2
Médicis, Catherine de, 3
Merged families, 96–97

Notices, 123–124
     to each other, 123
     to others, 124

Pensions, 43, 119
Postdissolution contracts, 130
Power of attorney, 100, 105
     enduring, 105
Prenuptial agreements, 22–43
     arbitrations in, 35
     careers and, 23
     checklist for, 29–36
          adoptions in, 34
          assets in, 31
          competency to enter
               into, 34
          day-to-day details in, 37

Prenuptial agreements (*Cont.*):
          escape clause in, 31
          and household expenses,
               32
          identification of parties
               to, 29
          income in, 31
          law governing, 35
          liabilities in, 31
          personal-conduct rules in,
               38–39
          property in, 32
          religious observance in,
               38
          residence included in, 30
          taxes in, 34
          vocational provisions in,
               32
          wills and, 33
     death and, 28, 33
     earnings and, 27
     effective date of, 29
     first marriages and, 22–23
     further instruments for, 29
     legal advice in, 29
     separate properties in, 27
     and subsequent marriages,
          26
     successors bound by, 29
     what law governs, 35
Presents:
     essentials for recovery of,
          17
     return of, 14–15
          at death of donee, 17
Property:
     separate, 27
          control of, 27
          death and, 28

Property (*Cont.*):
  transfers of, 98
  in whose name: bank
    accounts, 103
    businesses, 27
    securities, 104
Property settlement and
    separation agreements,
    107–128
  arbitration clause in, 121–
    122
  and changed conditions,
    117
  checklist for, 111–112
  children and, 115–117, 131
  death and, 119
  entire-contract, 123
  family dependents in, 116
  funding arrangements in,
    120
  income in, 113–114
  life insurance in, 119
  living apart and, 121
  mutual releases in, 121
  no-molestation commitment
    in, 121
  notices in, 123
  and pensions, 119
  in permanent separation,
    110
  property in, 113–114
  and remarriages, 117
  support payments in, 116
  and taxes, 120
  validity of, 108
Public officials, women as, 30

Quasi-marriages, 62

Same-sex marriages (*see*
    Homosexuals)
Separation agreements:
  permanent, 110
  temporary, 124–125
Social Security, 43, 90, 128
Statute of frauds, 4
Stepparent, monetary agree-
    ments with, 95
Subsequent marriages, pre-
    nuptial agreements for,
    26
Support money (*see* Alimony)

Taxes, 34, 98, 120
Transfers of property, 98
Trusts, 98–100
  Clifford trust, 99, 100
  in estate planning, 98
  inter vivos, 98
  testamentary, 98

Unilateral repudiation of
    betrothal contract, 10

Validity of prenuptial con-
    tracts, 108

Wedding, the 46
  (*See also* Marriage con-
    tracts)
Wills, 33, 71, 94